Dark Right
Batman Viewed From the Right

Edited by

Greg Johnson
&
Gregory Hood

Counter-Currents Publishing Ltd.
San Francisco
2018

Copyright © 2018 by Counter-Currents Publishing
All rights reserved

Cover image by Nathan Malone

Cover design by Kevin I. Slaughter

Published in the United States by
COUNTER-CURRENTS PUBLISHING LTD.
P.O. Box 22638
San Francisco, CA 94122
USA
http://www.counter-currents.com/

Hardcover ISBN: 978-1-940933-50-4
Paperback ISBN: 978-1-940933-51-1
E-book ISBN: 978-1-940933-52-8

Library of Congress Cataloging-in-Publication Data

Names: Johnson, Greg, 1971- editor. | Hood, Gregory, 1980- editor.
Title: Dark right : Batman viewed from the right / edited by Greg Johnson & Gregory Hood.
Description: San Francisco : Counter-Currents Publishing Ltd., 2018. | Includes bibliographical references and index.
Identifiers: LCCN 2017056694 (print) | LCCN 2018000090 (ebook) | ISBN 9781940933528 (e-book) | ISBN 9781940933504 (hardcover : alk. paper) | ISBN 9781940933511 (pbk. : alk. paper)
Subjects: LCSH: Batman films--History and criticism. | Motion pictures--Political aspects--United States. | Batman (Fictitious character)--Political aspects. | Batman (Fictitious character)--Social aspects. | Comic books, strips, etc.--United States--History and criticism. | Conservatism in literature. | Batman (Comic strip)--Political aspects.
Classification: LCC PN1995.9.B34 (ebook) | LCC PN1995.9.B34 D37 2017 (print) | DDC 791.43/651--dc23
LC record available at https://lccn.loc.gov/2017056694

Contents

1. Editors' Introduction—Gregory Hood
   & Greg Johnson ❖ 1

   ## The Dark Knight Trilogy

2. *Batman Begins*—Trevor Lynch ❖ 11
3. *The Dark Knight*—Trevor Lynch ❖ 15
4. *The Dark Knight Rises*—Trevor Lynch ❖ 27
5. The Order in Action: *The Dark Knight Rises*
   —Gregory Hood ❖ 39
6. Conservatism's League of Stupidity: Christopher Nolan as Fascist Filmmaker?
   —Gregory Hood & Luke Gordon ❖ 50
7. Gotham Guardian: Will the Real Batman Please Stand Up?—Jason Reza Jorjani ❖ 67
8. Superheroes, Sovereignty, & the Deep State
   —Greg Johnson ❖ 83
9. Caesar Without Gods—Christopher Pankhurst ❖ 95
10. A Dark Knight without a King—Will Windsor ❖ 105
11. The Ponderous Weight of the Dark Knight,
    —James J. O'Meara ❖ 116

    ## Batman vs. Superman

12. *Man of Steel*—Trevor Lynch ❖ 126
13. Superman & the White Christ: *Man of Steel*
    —Gregory Hood ❖ 131
14. *Batman v Superman: Dawn of Justice*
    —Trevor Lynch ❖ 141
15. *Justice League*—Trevor Lynch ❖ 146

COMICS & GRAPHIC NOVELS

16. The Alt Knight: A Retrospect of Frank Miller's *Dark Knight Returns* for the Current Year—Zachary O. Ray ❖ 150

17. *Batman: The Dark Knight Returns*—Trevor Lynch ❖ 161

18. Batman & the Joker—Jonathan Bowden ❖ 165

19. *Arkham Asylum*: An Analysis—Jonathan Bowden ❖ 169

20. Batman as Comedy—Spencer J. Quinn ❖ 176

TIM BURTON'S BATMAN MOVIES

21. Tim Burton's *Batman*: Putting the Gothic into Gotham—David Yorkshire ❖ 181

22. *Batman Returns*: An Anti-Semitic Allegory?, —Andrew Hamilton ❖ 191

Index ❖ 203

About the Authors ❖ 217

"Why are You People Here?"
Editors' Introduction

Sometimes, an idea contains within itself the seeds of its own subversion. Sometimes, so can a superhero.

Globalism necessarily requires the eradication of all organic cultures, traditions, and identities. However, deracinating mankind obviously creates a void. Even the most atomized individual desires some kind of a mythos, some image of the transcendent and that which is above. In a world (as the trailer voice guy would intone) where culture has been replaced by consumerism, where "God is dead" and reality is experienced on a screen, the closest glimpse most people have of the sublime is a superhero.

Superheroes are archetypes by which Consumerist Man interprets his reality. Sometimes, as in the case of Thor, a modern superhero is literally the cheapened, commodified, bastardized version of what entire peoples once adored as gods. Yet no superhero, no archetype, is quite so complex and yet so popular as Batman.

What makes Batman so appealing is that he is not really a "superhero" in the classic sense. He is not an alien, a god, or the recipient of special powers from a freak accident. He is an ordinary man who has transformed himself into something greater. The Christopher Nolan trilogy emphasizes this characteristic of Batman. As Bruce Wayne's mentor *cum* nemesis Ra's al Ghul counsels, "If you make yourself more than just a man, if you devote yourself to an ideal, and if they can't stop you, then you become something else entirely . . . legend."

And because in theory, anyone can choose to undertake this transformation, Batman can outlive Bruce Wayne himself. As Wayne tells Officer John "Robin"

Blake in *The Dark Knight Rises*, "The idea was to be a symbol, Batman could be anybody."

Or can it? Bruce Wayne is, after all, no ordinary man. As the mob boss Falcone sneers, "You're Bruce Wayne, the prince of Gotham, you'd have to go a thousand miles to meet someone who didn't know your name!" Wayne has all but unlimited financial resources and social connections. His butler and assistant Alfred Pennyworth is a veteran of the British SAS. His ownership of Wayne Enterprises gives him access to weapons and technology far superior to anything the Gotham police possess. It's true "anyone" can be Batman only in the same way "anyone" can be a billionaire.

Yet even with all of Bruce Wayne's advantages, even with the catalyst of his parents' murder, he would not have become Batman without the intervention of an Order. At least in the Nolan trilogy, the same institution which shaped Batman is his greatest foe, the League of Shadows. The League takes its values not from American capitalism or Thomas Wayne's vague *noblesse oblige* but a sense of a cosmic order, a desire to pursue "true justice." When we first find Bruce Wayne in *Batman Begins*, he is "truly lost," uselessly brawling with common criminals in a desperate quest for meaning. Ra's al Ghul rescues him from what surely would have been a short, pointless life, offering him a "path." After obtaining a blue flower, a symbol of trial similar to the white *Edelweiß* the German *Gebirgsjäger* use to this day, Wayne is initiated in a quasi-mystical fashion. He will serve True Justice, by destroying Gotham.

Yet Wayne shies away at this critical moment. He refuses to take the life of a murderer, saying he should be tried in a court. Ra's al Ghul protests, asking, rightly, why trust should be placed in "corrupt bureaucrats" as a credible source of authority. Wayne does not answer at the time, but the rest of Nolan's Dark Knight Trilogy, and the entire Batman mythos more broadly, is an answer to that question.

Underneath the corruption and crime, there is an inherent goodness to the people of Gotham city. If the terror under which they live can be lifted, the people will redeem their city. Wayne, reborn as "Batman," will transgress the law in order to restore the law, at the price of never being welcomed back into the society he saves, like John Wayne's character in *The Searchers*.

The spectacular villains Batman battles over the course of the series—Ra's al Ghul, Scarecrow, the Joker, Bane—conceal the reality that the source of corruption the Caped Crusader is fighting is simply the mafia. Gotham is a corrupt town, where justice can be bought and where police are inseparable from criminals. Like a revolutionary who embraces "propaganda of the deed," Batman's inhuman appearance and mythical reputation is designed to shock the common people of Gotham into anger against the rather mundane corruption which plagues it.

The point of Batman is to achieve a world where Batman is no longer necessary. This is why Batman's first ally is James Gordon, a rare honest cop on the beat (albeit one who won't "rat" on his corrupt colleagues). This is why Bruce Wayne thinks his mission is complete with the rise of Harvey Dent.

But as the Joker tells Batman in *The Dark Knight*, "You've changed things." You can't go back to the way things used to be, to the mundane, once you've introduced the extraordinary and the heroic. If law and order must be represented by the superhuman, so must villainy must be represented by the demonic. Even though Batman initially emerged to combat organized crime, the syndicate which ruled Gotham at the beginning of the series is practically irrelevant throughout the trilogy except as background.

Ultimately, Nolan's trilogy is a mediation on the nature of civic order. In the first film, *Batman Begins*, Bruce Wayne is transformed by the League of Shadows into Batman, but rejects the League's Traditionalist vision of "True Justice" in favor of a reformist approach. Like his father, Bruce Wayne wants to save Gotham, not see it brought to destruction in order to serve "balance." Batman's triumph over Ra's al Ghul suggests this is possible, as Gordon rises in power at the police department and ordinary people begin stepping forward to fight corruption.

In *The Dark Knight*, Batman's theory is challenged by the Joker, who begins tearing apart Gotham's power structure from the inside. Instead of corruption, the Joker brings chaos, which, though terrifying, is also enticing. "And you know the thing about chaos—it's fair," as he puts it.

Batman's ethos is challenged on two levels. First, his premise that ordinary people are good is challenged by the Joker's actions, as the villain forces them to choose between morality and survival. Second, Batman's faith in the system, and in the system's best representative, Harvey Dent, is challenged by the Joker's successful effort to mentally destroy him. What's more, Batman himself is irreparably damaged, as Rachel Dawes, his escape route to a "normal," post-Batman life, is killed.

These are deep themes, but the screenwriters blink rather than confronting the full ramifications of the Joker's actions in this film. As Trevor Lynch notes in his review, rather than responding with defiance or at least survival instinct, the people of Gotham react with paralysis and cowardice to the Joker. After presenting us with a brilliant character like the Joker (perfectly portrayed by the late Heath Ledger), we somehow end up with Batman growling the line, "The people of this city just showed you that it's full of people ready to believe in good." *Barney & Friends* couldn't pull of that line, let alone Nolan's "dark" Batman.

Yet the film closes on a stronger note. Harvey Dent, the exemplar of the System, is driven to madness and evil by the Joker. He even ends up threatening the life of a child. Batman saves the day, but as the Joker points out, if the people of Gotham learn their shining knight is a monster, "Two-Face," their spirits will be truly broken. To avoid this, Gordon and Batman choose to perpetuate a noble lie, like Plato advised. Batman will take the blame for Dent's crimes, Dent's reputation will be preserved, and his legend will justify the sweeping crackdown on organized crime the city needs. Peace will come at the price of a lie. Batman will retire, not to a normal life, but to bitter seclusion, treasuring the memory of Rachel Dawes.

The genius of the third film in the trilogy is that it directly challenges the moral of the second film and provides context for interpreting the entire series. The League of Shadows returns, led by the onetime outcast Bane. Bane is in some sense more honest even than Ra's al Ghul, who initially rejected him for personal reasons. In contrast, Bane seems to have subordinated his entire identity to a sense of mission. As he puts it, "No one cared who I was till I put on the mask." Ra's al Ghul's unchosen heir wields the most powerful weapon of all—truth. He confronts the public with the terrible reality of Harvey Dent, of how their elected leaders betrayed their trust, and how their entire social order is built on a lie. Revolution is the result.

Bruce Wayne is ill-suited to meet this new challenge. He is shattered by Alfred's revelation Rachel had chosen Harvey Dent over him. He is out of practice and overconfident. Most importantly, he misunderstands the nature of his foe, thinking Bane is someone just like all the others he has defeated.

Yet he's not. Conservative critics misinterpreted this film, believing Bane was operating as a Leftist. Yet Bane directly tells us his egalitarianism is a cruel illusion for the people of Gotham—"I will feed its people hope to torture their souls." In the first film, Ra's intends to drug the population of Gotham in order to create the spectacle of one of America's greatest cities tearing itself apart. In the finale, Bane offers something even more intoxicating, the dream of equality. The people will go mad voluntarily, not because they are on drugs.

But it's all an illusion. Bane knows it will fail. And after Gotham's people have shown themselves to be animals, the crabs pulling their fellows back down into the bucket, he'll destroy the city anyway.

Bane "breaks" Batman in combat. But as in the first film, Batman rebuilds himself and climbs out of the pit, symbolically reborn, remade. He defeats Bane, only to find it is Talia, Ra's al Ghul's daughter, a woman he thought he cared for, who is the true mastermind of the plot. But in the end, Batman still saves Gotham—with the indispensable help of Selina Kyle ("Catwoman," though she is never referred to as such). Kyle is a cynic who also comes to believe in saving Gotham, with all its imperfections.

Batman "dies" saving the city and is remembered as a hero, with Officer Blake ("Robin") set up as an heir. Bruce Wayne fulfills Alfred's dream of laying down the mask and moving on, living a new life accompanied by Selina Kyle. And contrary to theories online, it's very clear that this is the true ending, not just Alfred's fantasy. Wayne is alive, happy, and, finally, free.

Yet what message do we take away from all this? Bane has become something of an icon among the Alt Right, his utterances memes and catchphrases. In a way, Bane's view is ultimately proven over the course of the film, not Batman's. After all, Bane does prove Gotham, given "freedom," voluntarily chooses madness. It's significant that the only kind of law which exists in the final film is that dispensed by Dr. Jonathan Crane ("Scarecrow"), the only villain who appears in every film, a psychiatrist who is mad himself. What's more, through Bruce Wayne triumphs in the end, he does not get to live in peace as the "prince of Gotham." He fakes his own death and flees. Alfred says in the third film that perhaps it is time for the truth to have its day. But Bruce Wayne ultimately can only escape through another lie. And the suggestion that "Robin" will take up his mantle serves as a proof the System is still, even after all these deaths and sacrifices, incapable of preserving itself absent the intervention of extraordinary men who work outside it.

In that sense, one wonders if the League of Shadows is simply to be proven correct in the end. Dr. Thomas Wayne, through his charities and industry, tries to save Gotham, only to be shot down by a thug. His death inspires the rich to at least put some money towards their city, but it doesn't prevent Gotham from falling into corruption. Bruce Wayne, "Batman," liberates the city from the mob, the Joker, and the League at terrible cost, and he must ultimately leave the city to keep what's left of his sanity. And it is implied "Robin" will have to make the same sacrifices. The Wayne family legacy, Wayne Manor itself, becomes a home for orphans, perhaps a worthy endeavor, but something which would have prevented the creation of "Batman" had it happened after the death of Thomas Wayne. In other words, all these heroics ultimately serve only to unmake themselves. The superhero destroys himself to create a world where no one is extraordinary. He sacrifices all to save a System incapable of functioning on its own.

The Nolan Batman trilogy is thus really one long debate between "conservatives" and "traditionalists" or "conservative revolutionaries." Heroic conservatives like

Batman believe the System must be saved and see their role as doing what is necessary to save it. Traditionalists and conservative revolutionaries, like those in the League, believe Cosmic Order must be served and that terrible deeds now are justified to prevent corruption and devastation in the future. As for egalitarianism, well, it gets its shot under Bane's *faux*-revolution. Selina Kyle, who speaks gleefully about class warfare early on in *The Dark Knight Rises*, looks disgusted when she sees what Leftism really is in practice. It's no wonder she joins Bruce Wayne's Restorationist project and then flees with him to live abroad as an exile.

Beyond the Nolan trilogy and in his other incarnations, the Batman character always symbolizes the same essential message. The System is incapable of protecting itself. It thus requires the intervention of someone more than human, of an "ideal," of a person willing to take on the mantle of a criminal in order to serve the law.

Such a roguish hero is undeniably attractive. While someone like Superman almost always serves the established order, Batman lives by his own standards, his own vision of the good. Not surprisingly, "The Dark Knight" is usually seen as cooler than the "Big Blue Boy Scout." Batman also has a uniquely American appeal, as his heroic qualities come from his own efforts rather than inborn traits. Even his wealth can be excused; after all, every American considers himself a "temporarily embarrassed millionaire."

Yet there's a deeper question, one Bruce Wayne shies away from. If a System is inherently corrupt, if it can only be saved by violating it, why should extraordinary men sacrifice themselves to save it? Those who truly want to serve justice will destroy it and build something superior, not allow the decadent and evil to survive through their own heroism.

Perhaps Batman isn't the hero Gotham, or America,

needs or deserves. Perhaps Bane has something more to tell us about the nature of our collapsing civilization than "The World's Greatest Detective." And perhaps true heroism lies in forcing a "reckoning," not simply extending "the borrowed time" those who rule us have all been living on.

We suspect you feel the same. No? "Really? Then why are you people here?"

Why a collection of essays viewing Batman from the Right? The entire superhero genre is inherently anti-liberal, for even though superheroes generally fight for liberal humanist values, they do so outside the law. They are vigilantes. But vigilantism only becomes necessary when the liberal legal order fails to secure justice. This implies that, ultimately, we are not governed by laws, but by men.

But the character of Batman, particularly after being rebooted in Frank Miller's *The Dark Knight Returns* and developed in Christopher Nolan's Dark Knight Trilogy, is not just anti-liberal, but decidedly Right-wing and thus the topic of endless Right-wing rumination, interpretation, and meming. This collection skims off the best of this work, giving special attention to the visions of Nolan and Miller, but also exploring other films, comics, and graphic novels.

We wish to thank the contributors to this volume, plus John Morgan, Michael Polignano, James J. O'Meara, A. Graham, Jef Costello, Paul Kersey, J. S., Nathan Malone, and Kevin Slaughter for helping bring this book to press.

Gregory Hood & Greg Johnson
April 18, 2018

BATMAN BEGINS

TREVOR LYNCH

In *Batman Begins* (2005) and its sequel *The Dark Knight* (2008), director Christopher Nolan breaks with the campy style of earlier Batman films, focusing instead on character development and motivations. This makes both films psychologically dark and intellectually and emotionally compelling.

Nolan's casts are superb. I was disappointed to learn that David Boreanaz—the perfect look, in my opinion—had been cast as Batman right up until the part was given to Christian Bale. But it is hard to fault Bale's Batman. He may be too pretty. But he has the intelligence, emotional complexity, and heroic physique needed to bring Batman to life. (Past Batmans Adam West, Michael Keaton, and George Clooney were jokes, but Val Kilmer was an intriguing choice.)

Batman Begins also stars Michael Caine, Gary Oldman, Liam Neeson, Cillian Murphy, Ken Watanabe, Rutger Hauer, and Morgan Freeman as one of those brilliant black inventors and mentors for confused whites so common in science fiction. In *The Dark Knight*, Bale, Caine, Oldman, Murphy, and Freeman return, and the immortal Heath Ledger *is* the Joker.

Batman Begins falls into three parts. In the first part we cut between Bruce Wayne in China and flashbacks of the course that brought him there. I despise the cliché that passes for psychology in popular culture today, namely that a warped psyche can be traced back to a primal trauma. So I was annoyed to learn that young Bruce Wayne became obsessed with bats when he fell down a well and was swarmed by them, and that he became a crime-fighter because his wealthy parents were gunned down in front of him by a mugger. Haunted by these traumas, billionaire Bruce Wayne ended up dropping out of Princeton to immerse himself in the criminal underworld, eventually ending up in a brutal prison in Red China.

Wayne is released by the mysterious Mr. Ducard—played by the imposing and charismatic Liam Neeson—who oversees his training in a mysterious Himalayan fortress run by the "League of Shadows," an ancient order of warrior-ascetics led by Ra's al Ghul (Ken Watanabe). The League follows the Traditional teaching that history moves in cycles, beginning with a Golden Age and declining into a Dark Age, which then collapses and gives place to a new Golden Age. The mission of the League of Shadows is to appear when a civilization has reached the nadir of decadence and is about to fall—and then give it a push. (Needless to say, they do not have a website or a Facebook page. Nor can one join them by sending in a check.)

The League's training is both physical and spiritual. The core of the spiritual path is to confront and overcome one's deepest fears using a hallucinogen derived from a Himalayan flower. In a powerful and poetic scene of triumph, Bruce Wayne stands unafraid in the midst of a vast swarm of bats. The first time I watched this, I missed the significance of this transformation, which is an implicit critique of "trauma" psychology, for traumas are shown to be ultimately superficial compared with the heroic strength to stand in the face of the storm. It is, moreover, perfectly consistent with the conviction that nature is ultimately more powerful than nurture.

Bruce Wayne accepts the League's training but in the end rejects its mission. He thinks that decadence can be reversed. He believes in progress. He and Ducard fight. Ra's al Ghul is killed. The fortress explodes. Wayne escapes, saving Ducard's life. Then he calls for his private jet and returns to Gotham City.

In act two, Bruce Wayne becomes Batman. Interestingly enough, Batman is much closer to Nietzsche's idea of the "Superman" than the Superman character is. Superman isn't really a man to begin with. He just looks like us. His powers are just "given." But a Nietzschean superman is a man who makes himself more than a mere man. Bruce Wayne conquers nature, both his own nature and the world around him. As a man, he makes himself more than a man.

But morally speaking, Batman is no *Übermensch*, for he remains enslaved by the sentimental notion that every human life has some sort of innate value. He does not see that this morality negates the worth of his own achievement. A Batman can only be suffered if he serves his inferiors. Universal human rights—equality—innate dignity—the sanctity of every sperm: these ideas license the subordination and ultimately the destruction of everything below—or above—humanity. They are more than just a death sentence for nature, as Pentti Linkola claims. They are a death sentence for human excellence, high culture, anything in man that points above man.

Of course Batman's humanistic ethic has limits, particularly when he makes a getaway in the Batmobile, crushing and crashing police cars, blasting through walls, tearing over rooftops. Does Bruce Wayne plan to reimburse the good citizens of Gotham, or is there a higher morality at work here after all?

In act two, Batman begins to clean up Gotham City and uncovers and unravels a complex plot. In act three, we learn who is behind it: the League of Shadows. We learn that Neeson's character Ducard is the real Ra's al Ghul, and he and the League have come to a Gotham City tottering on the brink of chaos—to send it over the edge. Of course Batman saves the day, and Gotham is allowed to limp on, sliding deeper into decadence as its people lift their eyes towards the shining mirages of hope and eternal progress that seduce and enthrall their champion as well.

Batman Begins is a dark and serious movie, livened with light humor. It is dazzling to the eye. The script was co-authored by Christopher Nolan and Jewish writer-director David Goyer. There are a few politically correct touches, such as Morgan Freeman (although I find it impossible to dislike Morgan Freeman) and the little fact that one of Wayne's ancestors was an abolitionist, but nothing that really stinks.

Batman Begins touches on many of the themes that I discerned in my reviews of Guillermo del Toro's *Hellboy* and *Hellboy II*.[1] Again, the villains seem to subscribe to the Traditionalist, cyclical view of history; they hold that the trajectory of history is decline; they believe that we inhabit a Dark Age and that a Golden Age will dawn only when the Dark Age is destroyed; and they wish to lend their shoulders to the wheel of time. That which is falling, should be pushed. The heroes, by contrast, believe in progress. Thus they hold that a better world can be attained by building on the present one.

This is a rather elegant and absolutely radical opposition, which can be exploited to create high stakes dramatic conflict. What fight can be more compelling than the people who want to destroy the world versus the people who want to save it?

This raises the obvious question: Who in Hollywood has been reading René Guénon and Julius Evola—or, in the case of *Hellboy*, Savitri Devi and Miguel Serrano? For somebody inside the beast clearly understands that a weaponized Traditionalism is the ultimate revolt against the modern world.

Counter-Currents/*North American New Right*,
September 23, 2010

---

[1] In *Trevor Lynch's White Nationalist Guide to the Movies*, ed. Greg Johnson (San Francisco: Counter-Currents, 2012).

THE DARK KNIGHT

TREVOR LYNCH

In my review of Christopher Nolan's *Batman Begins*, I argued that the movie generates a dramatic conflict around the highest of stakes: the destruction of the modern world (epitomized by Gotham City) by the Traditionalist "League of Shadows" versus its preservation and "progressive" improvement by Batman.

I also argued that Batman's transformation into a Nietzschean *Übermensch* was incomplete, for he still accepted the reigning egalitarian-humanistic ethics that devalued his superhuman striving and achievements even as he placed them in the service of the little people of Gotham.

This latent conflict between an aristocratic and an egalitarian ethic becomes explicit in Nolan's breath-taking sequel *The Dark Knight*, which is surely the greatest supervillain movie ever. (The greatest superhero movie has to be Zack Snyder's *Watchmen*.)

PHILOSOPHIZING WITH DYNAMITE

The true star of *The Dark Knight* is Heath Ledger as the Joker. The Joker is a Nietzschean philosopher. In the opening scene, he borrows Nietzsche's aphorism, "Whatever doesn't kill me, makes me stronger," giving it a twist: "I believe whatever doesn't kill you, simply makes you . . . *stranger.*" Following Nietzsche, who philosophized with a hammer, the Joker philosophizes with knives as well as "dynamite, gunpowder, and . . . gasoline!"

Yes, he is a criminal. A ruthless and casual mass murderer, in fact. But he believes that "Gotham deserves a better class of criminal, and I'm going to give it to them. . . . It's not about money. It's about sending a message. Everything burns." In this, the Joker is not unlike another Nietzschean philosopher, the Unabomber, who philosophized with explosives because he too wanted to send a message.

The Joker's message is the emptiness of the reigning values. His goal is the transvaluation of values. Although he initially wants to kill Batman, he comes to see him as a kindred spirit, an alter ego: a fellow superhuman, a fellow freak, who is still tragically tied to a humanistic morality. Consider this dialogue:

> **BATMAN**: Then why do you want to kill me?
> **THE JOKER**: I don't want to kill you! What would I do without you? Go back to ripping off mob dealers? No, no, NO! No. You . . . you . . . complete me.
> **BATMAN**: You're garbage who kills for money.
> **THE JOKER**: Don't talk like one of them. You're not! Even if you'd like to be. To them, you're just a freak, like me! They need you right now, but when they don't, they'll cast you out, like a leper! You see, their morals, their code, it's a bad joke. Dropped at the first sign of trouble. They're only as good as the world allows them to be. I'll show you. When the chips are down, these . . . these civilized people, they'll eat each other. See, I'm not a monster. I'm just ahead of the curve.

The Joker may want to free Batman, but he is a practitioner of tough love. His therapy involves killing random innocents, then targeting somebody Batman loves.

DEATH, AUTHENTICITY, & FREEDOM

The basis of the kinship the Joker perceives between himself and Batman is not merely a matter of eccentric garb. It is their relationship to death. The Joker is a bit of an existentialist when it comes to death: "in their last moments, people show you who they really are." Most people fear death more than anything. Thus they flee from it by picturing their death as somewhere "out there," in the future, waiting for them. But if you only have one death, and it is somewhere in the future, then right now, one is immortal. And immortal beings can afford to live foolishly and inauthentically. People only become real when they face death, and they usually put that off to the very last minute.

The Joker realizes that there is something scarier than death, and that is a life without freedom or authenticity.

The Joker realizes that mortality is not something waiting for him *out there* in the future. It is something that he carries around *inside him* at all times. He does not need a *memento mori*. He feels his own heart beating.

Because he knows he can die at any moment, he *lives* every moment.

He is *ready* to die at any moment. He accepts Harvey Dent's proposal to kill him based on a coin toss. He indicates he is willing to blow himself up to deter the black gangster Gambol—and everybody believes him. He challenges Batman to run him down just to teach Batman a lesson.

In his mind, the Joker's readiness to die at any moment may be his license to kill at any moment.

The Joker can face his mortality, because he has learned not to fear it. Indeed, he has come to love it, for it is the basis of his inner freedom. When Batman tries to beat information out of the Joker, he simply laughs: "You have nothing, nothing to threaten me with. Nothing to do with all your strength." Batman is powerless against him, because the Joker is prepared to die.

The Joker senses, perhaps mistakenly, that Batman could attain a similar freedom.

What might be holding Batman back? Could it be his

conviction of the sanctity of life? In *Batman Begins*, Bruce Wayne breaks with the League of Shadows because he refuses the final initiation: taking another man's life. Later in the movie, he refuses to kill Ra's al Ghul (although he hypocritically lets him die). In *The Dark Knight*, Batman refuses to kill the Joker. If that is Batman's hang-up, the Joker will teach him that one can only live a more-than-human life if one replaces the love of mere life with the love of liberating death.

LESSONS IN TRANSVALUATION

Many of the Joker's crimes can be understood as moral experiments and lessons.

1. When the Joker breaks a pool cue and tosses it to Gambol's three surviving henchmen, telling them that he is having "tryouts" and that only one of them (meaning the survivor) can "join our team," he is opposing their moral scruples to their survival instincts. The one with the fewest scruples or the strongest will to survive has the advantage.

2. The Joker rigs two boats to explode, one filled with criminals and the other with the good little people of Gotham. He gives each boat the detonator switch to the other one, and tells them that unless one group chooses to blow up the other by midnight, he will blow up both boats. Again, he is opposing moral scruples to survival instincts.

The results are disappointing. The good people cannot act without a vote, and when they vote to blow up the other ship, not one of them has the guts to follow through. They would rather die than take the lives of others, and it is clearly not because they have conquered their fear of death, but simply from a lack of sheer animal vitality, of will to power. Their morality has made them sick. They don't think they have the right to live at the expense of others. Or, worse still, they all live at the expense of others. This whole System is about eating one another. But none of them will own up to that fact in front of others.

Batman interprets this as a sign that people "are ready to believe in goodness," i.e., that the Joker was wrong to claim that, "When the chips are down, these . . . these civilized people, they'll eat each other." The Joker hoped to put oversocialized people back in touch with animal vitality, and he failed. From a biological point of view, eating one another is surely healthier than going passively to one's death *en masse*.

3. The Joker goes on a killing spree to force Batman to take off his mask and turn himself in. Thus Batman must choose between giving up his mission or carrying on at the cost of individual lives. If he chooses to continue, he has to regard the Joker's victims as necessary sacrifices to serve the greater good, which means that humans don't have absolute rights that trump their sacrifice for society.

4. The Joker forces Batman to choose between saving the life of Rachel Dawes, the woman he loves, or Harvey Dent, an idealistic public servant. If Batman's true aim is to serve the common good, then he should choose Dent. But he chooses Dawes because he loves her. But the joke is on him. The Joker told him that Dawes was at Dent's location, so Batman ends up saving Dent anyway. When Batman tells the Joker he has "one rule" (presumably not to kill) the Joker responds that he is going to have to break that one rule if he is going to save one of them, because he can save one only by letting the other die.

5. As Batman races towards the Joker on the Batcycle, the Joker taunts him: "Hit me, hit me, come on, I want you to hit me." The Joker is free and ready to die at that very moment. Batman, however, cannot bring himself to kill him. He veers off and crashes. The Joker is willing to die to teach Batman simply to kill out of healthy animal anger, without any cant about rights, due process, or other

moralistic claptrap.

6. Later in the film, Batman saves the Joker from falling to his death. He could have just let him die, as he did Ra's al Ghul. The Joker says:

> Oh, you. You just couldn't let me go, could you? This is what happens when an unstoppable force meets an immovable object. You are truly incorruptible, aren't you? . . . You won't kill me out of some misplaced sense of self-righteousness. And I won't kill you because you're just too much fun. I think you and I are destined to do this forever.

Again, one has the sense that the Joker would have been glad to die simply to shake Batman out of his "misplaced sense of self-righteousness."

At the risk of sounding like the Riddler:

> **Q:** What do you call a man who is willing to die to make a philosophical point?
> **A:** A philosopher.

Materialistic versus Aristocratic Morals

Modern materialistic society is based on two basic principles: that nothing is worse than death and nothing is better than wealth. Aristocratic society is based on the principles that there are things worse than death and better than wealth. Dishonor and slavery are worse than death. And honor and freedom are better than wealth.

We have already seen that the Joker fears death less than an inauthentic and unfree life. In one of the movie's most memorable scenes, he shows his view of wealth. The setting is the hold of a ship. A veritable mountain of money is piled up. The Joker has just recovered a trove of the mob's money—for which he will receive half. Tied up on top of the pile is Mr. Lau, the money launderer who tried to abscond with it.

One of the gangsters asks the Joker what he will do with all his money. He replies: "I'm a man of simple tastes. I like dynamite, and gunpowder, and . . . gasoline." At which point his henchmen douse the money with gasoline. The Joker continues: "And you know what they all have in common? They're cheap." He then lights the pyre and addresses the gangster: "All you care about is money. Gotham deserves a better class of criminal, and I'm going to give it to them."

Aristocratic morality makes a virtue of transforming wealth into something spiritual: into honor, prestige, or beautiful and useless things. Trading wealth for spiritual goods demonstrates one's freedom from material necessity. But the ultimate demonstration of one's freedom from material goods is the simple destruction of them.

The Indians of the Pacific Northwest practice a ceremony called the "Potlatch." In a Potlatch, tribal leaders gain prestige by giving away material wealth. However, when there was intense rivalry between individuals, they would vie for honor not by giving away wealth but by destroying it.

The Joker is practicing Potlatch. Perhaps the ultimate put-down, though, is when he mentions that he is only burning *his share* of the money.

THE MAN WITH THE PLAN

Gotham's District Attorney Harvey Dent (played by Nordic archetype Aaron Eckhart) is a genuinely noble man. He is also a man with a plan. He leaves nothing up to chance, although he pretends to. He makes decisions by flipping a coin, but the coin is rigged. It has two heads.

The Joker kidnaps Harvey Dent and Rachel Dawes and rigs them to blow up. He gives Batman the choice of saving one. He races off to save Dawes but finds Dent instead. Dawes is killed, and Dent is horribly burned. Half his face is disfigured, and one side of his coin (which was in Rachel's possession) is blackened as well. Harvey Dent has become "Two-Face."

The Joker, of course, is a man with a plan too. Truth be told, he is a criminal mastermind, the ultimate schemer. (Indeed, one of the few faults of this movie is that his elaborate schemes seem to spring up without any time for preparation.) When the Joker visits Dent in the hospital, however, he makes the following speech in answer to Dent's accusation that Rachel's death was part of the Joker's plan.

> Do I really look like a guy with a plan? You know what I am? I'm a dog chasing cars. I wouldn't know what to do with one if I caught it. You know, I just . . . *do* things.
>
> The mob has plans, the cops have plans. . . . You know, they're schemers. Schemers trying to control their little worlds. I'm not a schemer. I try to show the schemers how pathetic their attempts to control things really are. . . . It's the schemers that put you where you are. You were a schemer, you had plans, and look where that got you. I just did what I do best. I took your little plan and I turned it on itself. Look what I did to this city with a few drums of gas and a couple of bullets. Hmmm?
>
> You know . . . You know what I've noticed? Nobody panics when things go "according to plan." Even if the plan is horrifying! If, tomorrow, I tell the press that, like, a gang banger will get shot, or a truckload of soldiers will be blown up, nobody panics, because it's all "part of the plan." But when I say that one little old mayor will die, *well then everyone loses their minds!*
>
> Introduce a little anarchy. Upset the established order, and everything becomes chaos. I'm an agent of chaos. Oh, and you know the thing about chaos?

It's fair!

The Joker's immediate agenda is to gaslight Harvey Dent, to turn Gotham's White Knight into a crazed killer. "Madness," he says, "is like gravity. All you need is a little push." This speech is his push, and what he says has to be interpreted with this specific aim in mind. For instance, the claim that chaos is "fair" is clearly *à propos* of Dent's use of a two-headed coin because he refuses to leave anything up to chance. (Chaos here is equivalent to chance.) Dent's reply is to propose to decide whether the Joker lives or dies based on a coin toss. The Joker agrees, and the coin comes up in the Joker's favor. We do not see what happens, but the Joker emerges unscathed, and Harvey Dent is transformed into Two-Face.

THE CONTINGENCY PLAN

But the Joker's speech is not merely a lie to send Dent over the edge. In the end, the Joker really isn't a man with a plan, and the clearest proof of that is that *he stakes his life on a coin toss*. Yes, the Joker plans for all sorts of contingencies, but he knows that the best laid plans cannot eliminate contingency as such. But that's all right, for the Joker embraces contingency as he embraces death: it is a principle of freedom.

The Joker is in revolt not only against the morals of modernity, but also its metaphysics, the reigning interpretation of Being, namely that the world is ultimately transparent to reason and susceptible to planning and control. Heidegger called this interpretation of Being the *"Gestell,"* a term which connotes classification and arrangement to maximize availability, like a book in a well-ordered library, numbered and shelved so it can be located and retrieved at will. For modern man, "to be" is to be susceptible to being classified, labeled, shelved, and available in this fashion.

Heidegger regarded such a world as an inhuman hell, and the Joker agrees. When the Joker is arrested, we find that he has no DNA or fingerprints or dental records on file. He has no name, no address, no identification of any kind. His clothes are custom made, with no labels. As Commissioner Gordon says, there's "nothing in his pockets but knives and lint." Yes, the system has him, but has nothing on him. It knows nothing about him. When he escapes, they have no idea where to look. He is a book without a barcode: unclassified, unshelved, unavailable . . . free.

For Heidegger, the way to freedom is to meditate on the origins of the *Gestell*, which he claims are ultimately mysterious. Why did people start thinking that everything can be understood and controlled? Was the idea cooked up by a few individuals and then propagated according to a plan? Heidegger thinks not. The *Gestell* is a transformation of the *Zeitgeist* that cannot be traced back to individual thoughts and actions, but instead conditions and leads them. Its origins and power thus remain inscrutable. The *Gestell* is an *"Ereignis,"* an event, a contingency.

Heidegger suggests that etymologically *"Ereignis"* also has the sense of "taking hold" and "captivating." Some translators render it "appropriation" or "enowning." I like to render it "enthrallment": The modern interpretation of Being happened, we know not why. It is a dumb contingency. It just emerged. Now it enthralls us. We can't understand it. We can't control it. It controls us by shaping our understanding of everything else. How do we break free?

The spell is broken as soon as we realize that the idea of the *Gestell*—the idea that we can understand and control everything—cannot itself be understood or controlled. The origin of the idea that all things can be understood cannot be understood. The sway of the idea that all things can be planned and controlled cannot be planned or controlled. The reign of the idea that everything is necessary, that everything has a reason, came about as sheer, irrational contingency.

The Joker seeks to break the power of the *Gestell* not merely by *meditating* on contingency, but by *acting from it*, i.e., by *being* an irrational contingency, by being an agent of chaos.

He introduces chaos into his own life by acting on whim, by just "doing things" that don't make sense, like "a dog chasing cars": staking his life on a coin toss, playing chicken with Batman, etc. When Batman tries to beat information out of the Joker, he tells him that "The only sensible way to live in this world is without rules."

Alfred the butler understands the Joker's freedom: "Some men aren't looking for anything logical, like money. They can't be bought, bullied, reasoned, or negotiated with. Some men just want to watch the world burn."

The Joker introduces chaos into society by breaking the grip of the System and its plans.

He is capable of being an agent of chaos because of his relationship to death. He does not fear it. He embraces it as a permanent possibility. He is, therefore, free. His freedom raises him above the *Gestell*, allowing him to look down on it . . . and laugh. That's why they call him the Joker.

In All Seriousness

I like the Joker's philosophy. I think he is right. "But wait," some of you might say, "the Joker is a monster! Heath Ledger claimed that the Joker was 'a psychopathic, mass murdering, schizophrenic clown with zero empathy.' Surely you don't like someone like that!"

But remember, we are dealing with Hollywood here. In a "free" society we can't suppress dangerous truths altogether. So we have to be immunized against them. That's why Hollywood lets dangerous truths appear on screen, *but only in the mouths of monsters:* Derek Vinyard in *American History X*, Travis Bickle in *Taxi Driver*, Bill the Butcher in *Gangs of New York*, Ra's al Ghul in *Batman Begins*, the Joker in *The Dark Knight*, etc.

We need to learn to separate the message from the messenger, and we need to teach the millions of people who have seen this movie (at this writing, the seventh biggest film of all time) to do so as well. Once we do that, the film ceases to reinforce the system's message and reinforces ours instead. That's what I do best. I take their propaganda and turn it on itself.

What lessons can we learn from *The Dark Knight*?

Batman Begins reveals a deep understanding of the fundamental opposition between the Traditional cyclical view of history and modern progressivism, envisioning a weaponized Traditionalism (the League of Shadows) as the ultimate enemy of Batman and the forces of progress.

The Dark Knight reveals a deep understanding of the moral and metaphysical antipodes of the modern world: the Nietzschean concept of master morality and critique of egalitarian slave morality, allied with the Heideggerian concept of the *Gestell* and the power of sheer irrational contingency to break it.

The Joker weaponizes these ideas, and he exploits Batman's latent moral conflict between Nietzschean self-overcoming and his devotion to human rights and equality.

In short, somebody in Hollywood understands who the System's most radical and fundamental enemy is. They know what ideas can destroy their world. It is time we learn them too.

Let's show these schemers how pathetic their attempts to control us really are.

Counter-Currents/*North American New Right*,
September 27, 2010

The Dark Knight Rises

Trevor Lynch

The Dark Knight Rises, the third and final film of Christopher Nolan's epic Batman trilogy, does not equal *The Dark Knight*—which was scarcely possible anyway—but it is a superb piece of filmmaking. It is a better film than *Batman Begins* and develops the characters and themes of both previous films into a tremendously satisfying and deeply moving conclusion.

Christian Bale, Gary Oldman, Michael Caine, Morgan Freeman, and Cillian Murphy reprise their roles from the earlier films. Michael Caine steals the film whenever he appears on screen. New cast members include ravishing minx Anne Hathaway as the Catwoman, the hulking, charismatic Tom Hardy as Batman's nemesis Bane, Marion Cotillard as Miranda Tate/Talia, and Joseph Gordon-Leavitt (the least Jewish-looking Jew since William Shatner) as (Robin) John Blake.

Aside from Hans Zimmer's insipid and forgettable score, this is a superbly made film, artistically and technically. It would be a shame if people did not see *The Dark Knight Rises* in theaters because of a madman's shooting rampage on opening night in Aurora, Colorado. (Many of the audience members in Aurora demonstrated, by the way, that heroism is not just for the movies.) You need to see this film on the big screen. Lightning doesn't strike twice, right?

Although I will discuss isolated elements of the plot, including the epilogue, I will say only this about the plot as a whole: the League of Shadows returns to destroy Gotham, and Batman returns to stop them. What I wish to focus upon are the larger themes of the movie, particularly those that run through the whole trilogy. The continuities between *Batman Begins* and *The Dark Knight Rises* are easy to see, since the League of Shadows is Batman's opponent in both movies. The continuities between *The Dark Knight* and the rest of the series are not so obvious, but they are deep and important.

TRADITIONALISM

In *Batman Begins*, the young Bruce Wayne is rescued from a brutal prison in China by Henri Ducard a.k.a. Ra's al Ghul (Arabic for "head of the demon," played by Liam Neeson), a member of the League of Shadows, a secret brotherhood of warrior-initiates whose headquarters is somewhere high in the Himalayas.

The League of Shadows believes in the Traditional view of history. History moves in cycles, and its trajectory is decline. A historical cycle begins with a Golden Age or Age of Truth (Satya Yuga) in which mankind lives in harmony with the cosmic order. As mankind falls away from truth, however, society declines through Silver and Bronze Ages to the fourth and final age: the Iron or Dark Age (Kali Yuga), which dissolves of its own corruptions, after which a new Golden Age will arise.

The purpose of the League of Shadows is to hasten the end of the Dark Age and the dawn of the next Golden Age. Thus when a civilization is falling, they appear to give it a final push into the void: Rome, Constantinople, and now Gotham. And in every case, these are not mere cities, but cities that stand for entire civilizations. Thus the League of Shadows is here to destroy nothing less than the whole modern world.

In *Batman Begins*, the League of Shadows trains Bruce Wayne as an initiate, but he rebels before his final test and flees back to Gotham, where he reinvents himself as Batman. The League, however, follows him to Gotham to destroy the city, which is rife with corruption and decadence. Batman defeats them and kills Ra's al Ghul, but in *The Dark Knight Rises*, the League of Shadows returns under new leadership to finish the job.

"Do you wanna know how I got these scars?"

When the League of Shadows finds Bruce Wayne, he is a young man almost at the end of the road to self-destruction. Wayne is destroying himself due to his inability to deal with the scars of his past. His primal traumas include seeing his parents murdered by a mugger, as well as an inordinate fear of bats.

In addition to rigorous physical training, the League of Shadows also involves spiritual initiation. One such exercise involves the use of a hallucinogen derived from a Himalayan flower to confront and overcome one's deepest fears.

Another exercise is to transcend the world's ruling morality—the egalitarian notion that all human beings have some sort of intrinsic value—by killing a man. We are told he is a murderer and deserving of death. But Wayne thinks that even a murderer has value and thus deserves more than mere summary justice. He has rights to due process. So Wayne balks at this test and ends up killing quite a few members of the League of Shadows in the process. But he has no trouble with that, because they are "bad" people who don't believe in due process and the American way.

When Bruce Wayne returns to Gotham, he is an incomplete initiate. He has overcome the traumas of his past, giving him superhuman courage. His training in martial arts has given him superhuman abilities. But he has not rejected egalitarian humanism. He still subjects himself to the conventional morality. He is, in short, a superhero: a superhuman being who lives to serve his inferiors out of a sentimental sense of humanity.

Now this might not be such a bad thing, if the people

he served actually looked up to him and honored him as their superior. But they are egalitarians too, thus they resent their superiors, even if they are their benefactors.

In *The Dark Knight*, the Joker is a portrait of a fully achieved *Übermensch*. (Remember that Hollywood only allows superior men to appear as monsters, because to people today, they *are* monsters.) Like Batman, the Joker has overcome the scars of his past—literal scars, in the case of the Joker. When the Joker tells people how he got his scars, he spins a new story each time. As James O'Meara brilliantly suggested, this shows that the Joker has overcome his past.[1] He tells different stories because, to him, it does not matter how he got his scars. He has transcended them—and, as we shall see, everything else in his past.

Unlike Batman, however, the Joker has also gone beyond egalitarian humanism. He is psychologically free from his past and morally free from the yoke of serving his inferiors. As I argued in my essay on *The Dark Knight*, the Joker's crimes need to be seen as moral experiments to break down Batman's commitment to egalitarian humanism.

The Joker has all the traits of a fully realized initiate, but he doesn't exactly seem to be a team player. But of course we don't know how the Joker came to be the way he is, because that is part of the past he has transcended.

In *The Dark Knight Rises*, eight years have passed since the death of Harvey Dent/Two-Face. Batman's final act of self-sacrifice for the city of Gotham was to accept responsibility for Two-Face's crimes in order to preserve Harvey Dent as a symbol of incorruptible commitment to justice. Batman has disappeared, but Gotham's organized crime problem has been solved by the Dent Act, which provides

---

[1] http://www.counter-currents.com/2011/03/andy-nowickis-the-columbine-pilgrim/

for the indefinite detention of criminals.

The lie has, however, taken its toll on its architects: Bruce Wayne and Commissioner Gordon. Commissioner Gordon has lost his wife and family. Bruce Wayne has hung up his Batman costume and lives in seclusion in Wayne Manor, in mourning for Rachel Dawes, who he thought was waiting for him even though she had chosen to marry Harvey Dent. Wayne Enterprises is in a shambles, defaulting on its obligations to its shareholders and the public at large.

In short, Bruce Wayne has returned to his state at the beginning of *Batman Begins*: he is destroying himself because he cannot deal with the traumas of his past, and he is dragging everyone else down with him. Wayne is not just psychologically crippled; he is also physically crippled, walking with a cane.

When the League of Shadows returns, Wayne gets a leg brace, dusts off his Batman costume, and goes out to fight them. But Alfred warns him that despite his technological crutches, he is spiritually and physically incapable of beating Bane, who fights with the strength of belief, the strength of an initiate in the League of Shadows. And Bruce Wayne is no longer an initiate.

Alfred is right. When Bane and Batman finally clash, Bane trounces Batman, twisting his spine and then casting him into a vast pit in some god-forsaken place in Central Asia. The pit is a prison. It is open to the surface, which adds to the torment of the prisoners, who can see the world above but cannot reach it. Only one person has ever managed to climb out. Many others have died trying.

In the darkness, Wayne has to physically and spiritually rebuild himself. It is a recapitulation of his original initiation with the League of Shadows. It also recapitulates the initiation of one of his opponents, who was born in the pit and eventually climbed out as a child. Wayne masters his fear again and escapes, rising from darkness to light, the cave to the real world: perennial symbols of spiritual initiation. In this case, however, Wayne masters fear not by suppressing it but by using it. By dispensing with the safety of the rope, he reactivates his fear and uses it as motive power to make the final leap.

Having been effectively re-initiated by the League of Shadows, Wayne is now able to fight and defeat them. The message could not be clearer: technology cannot make us superhuman without the underlying spiritual preparation of initiation.

INITIATION & SUPERHUMANISM

What is the connection between Nietzschean superhumanism, which is emphasized in *The Dark Knight*, and Traditionalist initiation, which is emphasized in the other two films?

I understand Traditionalism ultimately in terms of the nondualistic interpretation of Vedanta: the height of initiation is the mystical experience of the individual soul's identity with Being, the active principle of the universe. In our ordinary human consciousness, we experience ourselves as finite beings conditioned by other finite beings, including our traumas; these are our scars. When we experience our identity with Being, however, our finite bodies are infused with the active, creative, infinite power: the source of all things. This gives the initiate the power to overcome his merely finite, conditioned self, as well as other finite beings. Thus Traditionalists have their own supermen: the yogic adepts who attain magical powers (*siddhis*) through consciously experiencing their identity with Being.

Being is one, thus it is beyond all dualities, including the duality of good and evil. Thus the initiate who achieves mystical unity with Being rises beyond good and evil. He also rises beyond egalitarianism, since there is a fundamental difference between the initiated and the uninitiated. Finally, he rises above humanism, since he realizes that individual humans have no intrinsic worth or being. We are merely roles that Being plays for a while, masks that Being assumes and then discards. And if the initiate's role in the cosmic play is to negate millions of these nullities, what's the harm in that? Being itself cannot die, and its creative power is infinite, so there's always more where they came from.

In sum, on the nondualist Vedantic model, the culmination of initiation in a mystical experience of the identity of the self with Being leads to: (1) the infusion of superhuman powers, (2) the overcoming of external conditions, including one's past, (3) a view of the world beyond all dualities, including good and evil, and (4) the overcoming of egalitarian humanism.

Batman and the Joker display some of these traits, although nothing close to the essentially magical powers ascribed to yogic adepts. Batman, of course, never goes beyond good and evil, beyond egalitarian humanism. And the Joker, who has achieved moral liberation, does not display any superpowers, although he is remarkably accomplished.

"NOTHING IN HIS POCKETS BUT KNIVES AND LINT."

When the Joker is arrested in *The Dark Knight*, Commissioner Gordon is flummoxed: they don't know who he is. They can find no DNA, fingerprint, or dental records. They don't know his name or date of birth. His clothes are custom made, with no labels. As Gordon says, "There's nothing in his pockets but knives and lint."

If the would-be superman sometimes strives to overcome and forget his past, modern society means to keep us all tied to our pasts by compiling records. Of course mere bookkeeping cannot stop the inner spiritual transformation by which man becomes superman, rising above the conditioning of his past. But we are dealing with materialists here. Your karmic records are meaningless to them. But your tax returns and internet traffic are not.

In *The Dark Knight Rises*, Selina Kyle (Catwoman) is searching for a computer program called Clean Slate that will delete her from all existing computer records, allowing her to completely escape from her past. She craves the Joker's freedom. Batman offers to give her the program in exchange for her help. In the end, both she and Bruce Wayne seem to have used it to escape their pasts and start a new life together in Italy.

Of course, deleting all records of one's past is not the same thing as overcoming the past psychologically and existentially. That is possible only through a fundamental transformation of one's being. But once that transformation is in place, the technology sure can be useful.

"ALL YOU CARE ABOUT IS MONEY."

Contempt for money is another theme common to *The Dark Knight* and *The Dark Knight Rises*. In *The Dark Knight*, the Joker demonstrates his contempt for money by burning his share of a vast fortune.

In *The Dark Knight Rises*, some of Bane's best lines deal with money. His two most spectacular public attacks are on the stock exchange and a football game (as Gregory Hood puts it so memorably in the next essay in this collection: the bread and circuses of the decadent American empire).

In the stock exchange, one of the traders speaks to Bane as if he were a common criminal, and a moronic one at that: "We have no money here to steal." To which Bane replies, "Then why are you people here?"

When Bane breaks a deal with a businessman who has outlived his usefulness, the businessman protests that he has paid Bane a small fortune. "And that gives you power over me?" Bane asks.

Most commentators are somewhat confused about

Bane's attitude toward money, because he leads a Communist-style insurrection against the rich. But there are two critical perspectives one can take on money. Figuratively speaking, one can view it from above or from below. Those who criticize money from below are those who lack it and want it. Their primary motive is envy, which is not necessarily wrong. A hungry man has good reason to envy your bread. And he has good reason to hate you if you prefer to waste it rather than share it. The people who criticize money from below actually have a lot in common with the people they envy: all they care about is money, either getting it or keeping it.

Bane, however, criticizes money from above. His perspective is aristocratic, not egalitarian. He is an initiate, a spiritual warrior against decadence. He realizes there is something higher than money, and he feels contempt for those who are ruled by it, for those who think that money is the highest power in this world. He is, to use the Joker's phrase, "a better class of criminal."

Like the Joker, Bane is free of material concerns even as he masterfully manipulates the base, material world to fight for higher, spiritual aims. Like the Joker, Bane is not above using people who are only interested in money to further his spiritual aims. Thus Bane both makes deals with the rich and incites the envious mob to rise against them, all to hasten the destruction of Gotham.

THE GOOD LITTLE PEOPLE OF GOTHAM

In *The Dark Knight*, the Joker argues that the people of Gotham are only as good as the world allows them to be, and when the chips are down, "they'll eat each other." This sounds like a terrible insult, but from the Joker's perspective it is actually a form of optimism. Being willing to eat one another is a sign of animal vitality unrestrained by egalitarian humanist slave morality. The Joker claims that he is not a monster; he is just "ahead of the curve": meaning that he is already what the rest of Gotham would be if only they were "allowed" by society (or courageous enough to go there without society's permission).

The Joker rigs two boats to explode and gives the detonators to the people in the other boats. He tells them that if they blow up the other boat, he will let them live. If neither boat is destroyed by midnight, he will blow up both of them. One boat is filled with criminals and cops. The other is filled with the good little people of Gotham. In the end, however, neither group manages to blow up the other, and Batman prevents the Joker from destroying both.

Batman draws the false conclusion that the boats were filled with people who believe in goodness, whereas in fact they were merely too craven, decadent, and devitalized to do anything "bad," even to save their own lives. The Joker, it turns out, was a lot farther ahead of the curve than he thought.

In *The Dark Knight Rises*, Bane proves the Joker's point, but he shows that it will take nothing less than a revolutionary mob before the people of Gotham find the courage to eat each other, beginning with the rich. The revolutionary mob gives people permission to act atavistically. But beyond that, they have moral permission as well because, in the end, egalitarian altruism really is a kind of cannibal ethics.

The least convincing part of *The Dark Knight Rises* is the portrayal of the police as improbably idealistic and self-sacrificing. In *The Dark Knight*, the police force consists almost entirely of corrupt, gun-toting bureaucrats counting the days until their pensions kick in. In *The Dark Knight Rises*, Bane lures 3,000 police into the tunnels under Gotham and traps them there. When they finally break out, they charge *en masse* into battle armed only with their sidearms against Bane's heavily-armed fighters. I don't deny that it is possible to awaken such idealism, even in the most cynical public servant. But I needed to see some *reason* for such a dramatic transformation, perhaps something analogous to Bruce Wayne's transformation in his own underground prison.

Catwoman is motivated primarily by envy of the rich, but the revolution in Gotham has left her thoroughly disgusted. She tells Batman that as soon as she finds a way out, she is leaving. She does, however, linger for personal reasons: she wants to save Batman too. She urges him to follow, telling him that he has given everything for these people. He replies "Not everything, not yet." Then he apparently commits suicide to save the city. But in the end, we learn that Bruce Wayne was not willing to give his life for Gotham. But he was willing to give up Gotham and Batman for a life of his own.

The ending is enigmatic, but as I read it, Bruce Wayne has finally arrived at a higher level of initiation. Again, he has triumphed over his past, this time entirely, and he has used Clean Slate to erase all traces of his life and Catwoman's. He has also risen above egalitarian humanism. He no longer lives for his inferiors. He lives for himself, and he has found happiness with Catwoman, which is an interesting change, since it means he has decided to put his happiness above the mere fact that she is a wanted criminal.

Of course, in my eyes, the fact that Bruce Wayne has apparently chosen a private life makes him inferior to Bane. Yes, Wayne has ceased to serve those who are beneath him, but merely serving oneself is inferior to serving a cause that is greater than oneself, which is what Bane did.

TRUTH OR CONSEQUENCES

One of the most important new themes introduced in *The Dark Knight Rises* is the destructiveness of lies. Gordon and Wayne are both debilitated by the burden of the lies they told to protect the reputation of Harvey Dent. Wayne is also crushed by the loss of Rachel Dawes, which is made all the more painful because Alfred chose to conceal the fact that she had chosen to leave Bruce Wayne for Harvey Dent. Finally, near the end of the movie, Robin Blake lies to a group of orphans to give them hope, even though there really wasn't any. The common denominator is that all these lies are told altruistically, to protect people, and particularly "the people," from the truth. Lies are particularly necessary in statecraft, even at its highest and most disinterested. Lies are, of course, a form of bondage to society and the past. Thus they must be rejected by those who would be free, although the initiates seem quite willing to employ deception and violence for a higher cause.

The Left as the Vanguard of Nihilism

The Dark Knight Rises is an extremely Right wing, authoritarian, fascistic movie.

First of all, in this movie, both the good guys (Wayne, Gordon) and the bad guys (the League of Shadows) are united in their belief that Gotham is corrupt and decadent. In the earlier films, the good guys clearly believed that progress was possible. Now they are just looking for excuses to retire, because society no longer has anything to offer them. They have given without reward until their idealism has been extinguished and their souls have been completely emptied. They have become burned-out shells in thankless service to their inferiors.

Second, Nolan's portrayal of the Left is utterly unsympathetic: Leftist values are shown to be nihilistic. Thus promoting Leftism is a perfect tool for those who would destroy a society.

Third, and most trivially, the uncritical portrayal of the police would surely score high on the authoritarian personality inventory, although White Nationalists are not so naïve.

The Dark Knight Rises is a remarkable movie, a fitting conclusion to a highly entertaining and deeply serious and thought-provoking trilogy. As unlikely as it may seem, these films touch upon—and vividly illustrate—issues that are at the heart of the New Right/Radical Traditionalist critique of modernity. Tens of millions of young whites are eagerly watching and analyzing these films. Thus it is important for us to use these films to communicate our ideas.

Yes, Hollywood always puts our ideas in the mouths of psychotics in order to immunize people against them. But these ideas are one reason why the villains are always more interesting than Batman, who merely comes off as a tool.

I have suggested that these movies incorporate elements from Radical Traditionalism and Nietzschean superhumanism to generate maximum dramatic tension. What conflict could be more fundamental than the one between those who wish to destroy the world and those who wish to save it? That said, I cannot help wondering if Christopher Nolan also feels some sympathy for these ideas, although of course he would deny it. But whatever Nolan's ultimate sympathies, there is no question that somebody in Hollywood knows which ideas offer the most fundamental critique of the modern world. Isn't it time for White Nationalists to learn them as well?

Counter-Currents/*North American New Right*,
July 31, 2012

THE ORDER IN ACTION:
The Dark Knight Rises

GREGORY HOOD

The Dark Knight Rises is beyond Left and Right, beyond good and evil, beyond any frame of reference that this society can understand. Christopher Nolan's *Batman* trilogy closes with a vision of weaponized Traditionalism certain to be misunderstood by movie reviewers and talking heads who think in terms of Republicans versus Democrats. It's similarly beyond the grasp of fanboys playing compare and contrast with *The Avengers* or *Superman*.

That said, it's a comic book movie, it's a blockbuster, and the demands of the medium necessitate that Nolan cannot go all the way. The most interesting characters are, as always, the villains.

That said, there is something deeply unsettling at the heart of this film, a strange uneasiness that cannot be shaken even after applause fades, the credits roll, and the costumed audience tromps happily into the early morning after a midnight showing. The murder of 12 people at a premiere in Colorado throws a glare on the sickness at the heart of our own society, begs a comparison between the corruption of Gotham and the rot of our own post-America, and forces us to ask, "Is the fire rising?"

The film is utterly unintelligible without the other films in the trilogy. It begins with Gotham paying tribute to its fallen white knight Harvey Dent, who is remembered as an incorruptible crusader against injustice. The symbol also serves as the justification for Dent Act, which keeps the soldiers of organized crime behind bars without hope for parole. However, the fragile peace of Gotham is based on a lie: Batman accepted the blame for Harvey Dent/Two Face's killing spree at the end of *The Dark*

Knight. Gotham has stability, but it is the stability of a static and lifeless society, a soft but pervasive repression reminiscent of Brezhnev's Russia, with an explosion just below the surface.

The lie has taken its toll on both Commissioner Gordon and Bruce Wayne. Gordon is weary, tired, almost broken by the burden of having to live out the necessary falsehood. His victory over crime is hollow, his usefulness exhausted, and his civilian superiors already planning his replacement. In *The Dark Knight,* there is an agonizing moment when his wife Barbara is told that he has been killed, followed by a tearful reunion when his necessary deceit is revealed. By the beginning of this film, Barbara has embraced the noble equality offered the gentler sex in our enlightened time and abandoned him, of course taking the children with her. "Manning up" and doing what is necessary to save one's city and loved ones is ruthlessly punished by modernity, as it always is.

Wayne, meanwhile, has become a recluse, obsessing over his lost love Rachel Dawes, who he still believes was waiting for him. His great task of saving Gotham accomplished, Wayne is physically and emotionally crippled. Wayne's only project is the predictable endeavor of any good Hollywood superhero/tycoon: the pursuit of clean energy. He is assisted by Miranda Tate, a (seemingly) typical liberal do-gooder philanthropist, dreaming of sustainable development, and no doubt, helping the underprivileged, uplifting the oppressed, and doing it all from her drawing room. Unfortunately, Wayne learns that the fusion reactor they were developing could be turned into a weapon, so he shuts the project down, costing Wayne Enterprises millions. As the Joker points out in *The Dark Knight,* Wayne and Gordon are both "schemers," trying to "control their little worlds." As a result, they are trapped by their lies, their fears, and their insecurities.

One of the first signs that the peace is breaking is the

emergence of Selina Kyle (Anne Hathaway's Catwoman), a cat burglar seething with resentment against the privileged. Contemptuous of Bruce Wayne and other limousine liberals flattering themselves with their own altruism, Kyle seduces and steals from high society as an act of vengeance, but she is actually seeking an escape from her past. She removes a necklace from Bruce Wayne's safe, but more importantly, steals his fingerprints for an unknown use. While she thinks she is striking back at the decadent rich, she is actually being used as a pawn by a more dangerous and dedicated group with a higher end in mind than class warfare.

Their leader is Bane, a hulking but brilliant mercenary who was supposedly "excommunicated" from the League of Shadows. Having built an underground army (literally underground), Bane's plans are disrupted when Commissioner Gordon discovers their existence, ending up hospitalized. From his bedside, Gordon pleads for Batman to return. The League of Shadows, which trained Bruce Wayne and in many ways "made" Batman, is the Traditionalist Order headed formerly headed by Ra's al Ghul. Batman turned on the Order in spectacularly unconvincing fashion in the first film. Why Batman turned on his erstwhile creators remains unanswered in *The Dark Knight Rises*. Batman merely states that they were a bunch of "psychopaths," a strange claim coming from a man dominated alternately by childhood fears and long vanished pseudo-girlfriends.

Recognizing that Bruce is trapped by the past, Alfred reveals that Rachel had chosen Harvey Dent over him and that he had concealed it to spare Bruce pain. Alfred also pleads for Bruce to leave everything behind, pointing out Bane's obvious skill, strength, and training. Bruce refuses, seemingly hoping for death. Alfred confesses that he never wanted Bruce to come back to Gotham, as there was nothing for him there but pain, and confesses a fantasy of him living abroad, somehow having gotten beyond Gotham City. Alfred tearfully leaves Bruce Wayne's service, leaving Batman truly alone for the first time.

After a brief liaison with Miranda Tate, Bruce Wayne uses Selina Kyle to reach Bane, counting on Kyle being more than a mere criminal. He's wrong. He is betrayed and forced into a confrontation with Bane, who calls him "Mr. Wayne" (to Kyle's shock). Bane breaks him, defeating him in physical combat and snapping his spine, before throwing him into an open air prison below the earth. Crippled, Bruce Wayne will be forced to watch the suffering of Gotham while being taunted by the promise of freedom above.

With Batman removed, the League moves with startling swiftness to take over Gotham. A police raid into the sewers to capture Bane's forces backfires, and the police are trapped *en masse* below the earth. Bane uses his more materialistic pawns to capture Wayne Enterprises and seize the nuclear device Bruce inadvertently provided, as well as Batman's arsenal. Bane reveals the bomb's existence after an attack at a football game. He exposes Batman and Gordon's lies about Harvey Dent and gives Gotham to "the people," by freeing the "oppressed" criminals imprisoned by the Dent Act. The result is that Gotham becomes a kind of Paris Commune, with the possessions of the wealthy seized outright and dissidents condemned to death by Dr. Jonathan Crane (Scarecrow), the only villain who appears in all three movies, who returns as a revolutionary hanging judge.

Commissioner Gordon, fresh from the hospital, tries to rally what resistance he can. He is assisted by John Blake, an officer who has discovered the true secret of Batman's identity and wants him to return. The few above-ground police fail to win back the city, as an effort to smuggle in Special Forces from outside fails miserably.

Meanwhile, Batman recovers slowly underground. He

learns about the origins of Bane and his connection to the League of Shadows and Ra's al Ghul. To escape the prison, which only one other person (Bane) has done, he must climb out of the darkness and into the light, as the other trapped prisoners chant "Deshi Basara" (he rises). After several failures, Wayne is told that he can only escape if he climbs without a safety rope—meaning that another mistake will mean certain death. Wayne climbs and escapes, reborn as Batman. After saving Gordon, his fiery emblem announces his return to Gotham. He frees the police, and together Batman and his new army assault Bane's base of power at City Hall.

Batman manages to defeat Bane in their rematch, knocking off part of Bane's mask which delivers a gas that eases his chronic pain. At the moment of Batman's triumph, Miranda Tate plunges a dagger into him, revealing herself as Ra's al Ghul's daughter Talia and the real escapee of the prison. Bane was merely her guardian, who was injured defending her and expelled from the League because of his love for her. Talia attempts to trigger the bomb, but the mechanism has been disabled by Gordon, buying a few moments. She flees in one of the Tumblers (Batmobiles) to guard the bomb. Kyle appears and kills Bane with firepower from the Batpod, and together Batman, Kyle, and Gordon chase down the bomb. Talia is killed, but there is no way to disable the bomb. Thus Batman heroically flies the bomb over the ocean, where it detonates, apparently killing him but saving the city.

In the aftermath, Gotham memorializes Batman as its true hero. Bruce Wayne is remembered simply as a victim of the class violence. His true identity remains a secret, and most of his assets go to help underprivileged children. John Blake (whose real first name is revealed to be Robin) is given the coordinates of the Batcave in Wayne's will. Gordon, still Commissioner, finds a new Batsignal on the roof of the police station, suggesting Blake has taken up the mantle of the Batman. A heartbroken Alfred travels overseas. At a café, he suddenly looks up and nods, and the camera reveals Bruce Wayne and Selina Kyle. Bruce Wayne is no longer Batman, but he is still alive.

From the perspective of Bruce Wayne, the film has to end as it did. While there were rumors that Batman would be killed off, this "darker" ending would actually have been a cop out. Bruce Wayne's obsession with the Batman, with Rachel, and his own death wish show that he never learned to put suffering behind him. As Alfred points out, "You see only one end to your journey." Wayne has the characteristically American attitude that bad things cannot happen to good people, and that suffering is a vast departure from the way things ought to be. As a result, when something bad does happen, he can never move beyond it and becomes brooding and obsessive. The ability of Bruce Wayne to put down the mask and move beyond that Bat is necessary for his character to show growth, in some ways, the first real growth since the death of his parents.

What Wayne never goes beyond, and the movie never explains, are his continued sacrifices on behalf of Gotham. When Selina Kyle begs him to leave the city, pointing out that he's "given these people everything," Batman says, "not everything. Not yet." But who *are* these people? At the beginning of the film, when Bruce Wayne is brooding in his lair, he says to Alfred, "There's nothing for me out there." Instead of living, he is, in Alfred's words, "waiting for something bad to happen." Wayne is so disgusted with Gotham that he can't even bear to experience the peace he created at such a terrible price. Even his grand victory at the end of the trilogy is moving beyond Gotham, putting down the mantle of the Bat, and abandoning his own identity or anything that could tie him to a place that only brings him tragedy and pain.

The motives of the so-called villains are more substantial but would seem incomprehensible to anyone who hasn't seen *Batman Begins*. The most important role of the League of Shadows is to bring "balance" to civilization by destroying the centers of degeneracy when the rot has become too great. Like Constantinople or Rome before it, Gotham's time has come. While Batman managed to stop Ra's al Ghul, Bane and Talia have come to finish the job.

The Dark Knight Rises thus gives us a portrait of an Order in action. In the first scene, when Bane and his comrades seize a nuclear scientist from a CIA flight, Bane orders one of his men to stay behind. Addressing him as "brother," he explains that the enemy will expect to find at least one of their bodies in the wreckage. Seemingly unaffected, with a beatific smile, the League member asks, "Have we started the fire?" Bane nods and responds, "The fire rises." Bane routinely executes followers who fail and demands (and receives) complete willingness to die from his comrades. "Where do they find such people?" asks one awed observer.

The first two targets Bane attacks in Gotham are heavy with meaning.

The first is the stock exchange. As Bane takes control of the trading floor, a stockbroker pleads "There's no money here, there's nothing to rob!" Heavy with contempt, Bane responds, "Then why are you people here?" After completing the financial takeover of Wayne Enterprises, a non-League member accuses Bane of taking his money but not doing what he wants. Bane responds, "And this means you have power over me?" Realizing for the first time that he is confronting someone who has a higher end than money, the criminal asks "What are you?" prompting the response, "I'm Gotham's reckoning." Bane is not in it for money, and the League of Shadows looks with contempt at the vulgar traders and materialistic grubbers that constitute the supposed elite of the city. The League of Shadows is going to pull down the Kali Yuga in Gotham, whatever it takes.

At the same time, this is no egalitarian rant against "the rich." *The Dark Knight Rises* may be the most contemptuous treatment of egalitarianism ever produced on film. Needless to say, what passes for the American Right is not intellectually capable of understanding it, alternately complaining that Bane was created in order to attack Mitt Romney's finance capital firm or thinking it is a partisan attack on Occupy Wall Street in the name of millionaires like Romney and Bruce Wayne. Instead, *The Dark Knight Rises* is a direct attack on the idea that people can manage themselves.

Bane's second target is a football stadium hosting a pointless spectacle where a mostly white audience lives vicariously by watching mostly non-white players throw and chase a ball. The game begins with the singing of the national anthem, as if Nolan is telling us that pointless distractions *are* what America is all about today. If the stock exchange was the "bread" of this degenerate society, sports are the "circuses," and it is significant that Bane decapitates the political leadership of the city by blowing up the mayor's skybox at a sporting event. Bane takes away the diversions and forces the people to re-engage with History.

When Bane seizes control of Gotham, he claims that he is coming to "liberate" Gotham and tells the masses to "take control" of their city. He also frees the prisoners on the grounds that they are "oppressed," all *de rigueur* Left-wing talking points. The result is a complete breakdown of the city, with a criminal lunatic (Crane) serving as the focal point of power. The upper classes are destroyed, and the "people" instantly give themselves over to pointless consumption in a manner more degrading than the most spoiled trust fund baby. When one of Selina Kyle's erstwhile comrades celebrates that Wayne Manor now belongs to "everyone," Kyle is disgusted.

It turns out that Bane and Talia are planning on eventually destroying the entire city with a nuclear bomb anyway. While many conservative commentators claim that this is evidence that Bane (and thus Occupy Wall Street) is motivated by pure evil, the real message is far more subversive. Bane allows the city to live for a few months to show the world what Gotham's citizens are capable of. Libertarian ideologues and socialist revolutionaries get their chance, as the boot of the state is taken off, and the police are trapped underground. The result is an ugly, starving society ruled by the insane.

Bane delays destroying Gotham because he wants the world to watch how freedom failed. He gives the city a false hope by letting the people govern themselves, knowing they are not capable of it. This isn't the conquest of a healthy society—it's a laboratory experiment where the League of Shadows knows the outcome. A simple killing would be too merciful. The punishment "must be more severe." Only when the consequences are unmistakable and the corruption has been ripped out by the root will Bane give Gotham permission to die. Liberalism, classical or otherwise, is so self-evidently stupid that Bane gives it free reign knowing that it will fail spectacularly. Even more impressively, Bane and the other members of the League are willing to remain in the city when the bomb detonates, dying so that the corrupt world can be reborn. This is a creed of iron that demands the whole man in order to make him something more.

Batman is a more severe problem for the League because he is a product of the same Order as Bane, thus he is capable of withstanding his attack. Batman harnesses Traditionalism and the aristocratic (or even fascist) principle to save society from itself. Bane explicitly recognizes this. When Batman fights Bane the first time and uses his usual tricks, Bane comments, "Theatricality and deception are powerful weapons to the uninitiated . . . but we are initiated." When Batman is broken and left in the darkness, he is symbolically "killed," only to be reborn after he remakes himself and climbs into the light, a motif familiar to the ceremonies of many fraternal and religious orders. The use of ritualistic incantation is another indication that we are not watching a superhero with magical powers but the product of initiation.

But to what end? When Batman is recovering from his injuries in the darkness, he has a vision of Ra's al Ghul who taunts him that after years of complete sacrifice, the most that Bruce Wayne could achieve is a lie. At the end of the movie, once again, this is all that is achieved. Bruce Wayne did not die either as a victim of class warfare or as a hero of Gotham. He fled the city to pal around with Selina Kyle in Florence, enjoying lunches at fashionable restaurants. He cannot bear to live among the people he saved.

Wayne Manor is turned into a shelter for the children of the slums, postponing the inevitable end that the League was founded to hasten. Batman lives on through Robin John Blake, but the whole point of the trilogy was that Batman was supposed to be a temporary measure until the city could be returned to health and the "normal" system could govern without recourse to masked vigilantes.

Of course, this is the essential problem with Bruce Wayne's worldview. The return of the bat signal suggests that the extraordinary will always need to sacrifice themselves for the ordinary. Bane showed the true face of Gotham, but it was saved regardless, and it will continue to be saved by heroes that have to emerge from outside of society. Good men like Gordon are destroyed by the society that produces them, stripped of family and honor. Darker heroes like Batman find they can no longer even live in it. The best solution that can be offered is more charity from the rich, as if a Band-Aid can stanch a sucking chest wound. Batman's plea to save the city because there are "good" people is a pointless banality reminiscent of Judge Smails from *Caddyshack*. The League of Shadows presents a radical critique of society, and all Batman tells us is that we have to stand for "goodness" and not "badness."

The Batman trilogy poses deep questions about the nature of society, the importance of Radical Traditionalism, and the meaning of heroism. However, ultimately, it can only give the same answer as *The Avengers*: heroes are heroes precisely because they use their gifts and dedication to safeguard a world that is unworthy of them, preventing any attempts to turn it into something greater.[1] The Kali Yuga rolls on, the corrupt look up and shout "save us!," and heroes hasten to the call. But the sparks are there, and the conflagration is being prepared.

Counter-Currents/*North American New Right*,
July 22, 2012

---

[1] http://www.counter-currents.com/2012/05/the-avengers/

THE DARK RIGHT RISES:
CHRISTOPHER NOLAN AS FASCIST FILMMAKER?

GREGORY HOOD & LUKE GORDON

CONSERVATISM'S LEAGUE OF STUPIDITY
The egalitarian Left isn't just evil—it's boring. Unfortunately, the conservative "Right" doesn't have anything better to offer. It's not just true of politics—it's even true of their movie reviews.

The endless reinforcement of egalitarianism throughout the controlled culture means that to a great extent, every "superhero" film has the same plot. An extraordinary character is introduced, a challenge emerges to the liberal assumptions of modernity, and the hero, by humbling himself and accepting his responsibility to his inferiors, saves the day and preserves the sacred illusion of equality. The unintended result of this kind of culture is that the most interesting, intelligent, and genuinely substantive characters and ideas come from a film's supposed villains. Leftist commentators often recognize this and have genuinely insightful (or at least accurate) observations to make about a film's ideological content.

Perhaps the most subversive and overtly right wing movie to be made in many years was *The Dark Knight Rises,* the triumphant finale to director Christopher Nolan's epic Batman trilogy. The Left most recognized it for what it was. Noted Lefty policy wonk Matt Yglesias tweeted: "Had a lot of problems with *Dark Knight Rises* but it was sort of refreshing to see a balls-out insanely rightwing movie."[1] Andrew O'Hehir at *Salon* noted:

---

[1] https://twitter.com/mattyglesias/status/226709543688740864

It's no exaggeration to say that the "Dark Knight" universe is fascistic (and I'm not name-calling or claiming that Nolan has Nazi sympathies). It's simply a fact. Nolan's screenplay (co-written with his brother, Jonathan Nolan, and based on a story developed with David S. Goyer) simply pushes the Batman legend to its logical extreme, as a vision of human history understood as a struggle between superior individual wills, a tale of symbolic heroism and sacrifice set against the hopeless corruption of society. Maybe it's an oversimplification to say that that's the purest form of the ideology that was bequeathed from Richard Wagner to Nietzsche to Adolf Hitler, but not by much.[2]

They may not necessarily like fascism, or for that matter, anything that alludes to heroism or greatness, but at least we are talking about the same thing.

Of course, many "movement conservatives" miss the point of the movie entirely, seeing each new cultural phenomenon as another opportunity to bash the "Democrat Party" or give a eulogy about the glories of various purveyors of high fructose corn syrup and why they pay too much in taxes.

Thus, if we didn't have John Nolte and Ben Shapiro we'd have to make them up. The two writers at the late Andrew Breitbart's *Big Hollywood* somehow managed to view Nolan's climactic film as some sort of love letter to Goldman Sachs. Batman is pictured a capitalist hero presumably sent by the Cato Institute to protect the prosperous citizens of Gotham from the moral relativists of Occupy Wall Street. Comrade Bane is seen as the leader of evil Leftists, who probably also support Islamism, and is

---

[2] http://www.salon.com/2012/07/18/the_dark_knight_rises_christopher_nolans_evil_masterpiece/

nothing but a jealous nihilist who wants to bring about equality.

Shapiro gushes, "The entire film is an ode to traditional capitalism."[3] He condemns Bane's "communist-fascist" (?) regime and worries that Bane's evil "Leftist populism" sounds like Barack Obama. While this is idiotic, it's about par for the movement, and is still a bit more intelligent than Rush Limbaugh's charge that Bane was deliberately named to create sinister associations with Mitt Romney's "Bain Capital."[4] Just as Barack Obama can simultaneously be a Communist and a Nazi, Bane can be a liberal attack on Republicans and an obvious stand in for President Obama.

Where Ben Shapiro actually achieves a kind of conservative movement perfection is in celebrating that *The Dark Knight Rises* supposedly condemns green energy for being unprofitable, rips public-private partnerships for furthering Bane's plan, and is somehow pro-gun. (In a sentence, the "green energy" program works but Bruce Wayne doesn't want it weaponized and so halts it, the villain achieves his ends through totally private stock market manipulation, and Batman doesn't let Selina Kyle use guns.) It's so precisely wrong, reaching Bill Kristol and Dick Morris levels of factual absurdity, that it's beautiful. It's this kind of logic that gives us intellectuals who build entire careers explaining how Barack Obama's Democratic Party is racist against blacks and too pro-white, that Detroit, Camden, East Saint Louis, and Rochester were destroyed by white liberals, and that the problem with academia and the media is that they're anti-Semitic. You al-

---

[3] http://www.breitbart.com/Big-Hollywood/2012/07/20/Spoiler-Alert-TDKR-Most-Conservative-Movie-Ever
[4] http://www.politifact.com/truth-o-meter/statements/2012/jul/18/rush-limbaugh/rush-limbaugh-claims-link-between-batmans-bane-and/

most have to admire it.

Nolte meanwhile is so far off the mark with his review and his responses that it's difficult to believe he saw the movie. He charges that Bane is simply motivated by jealous nihilism simply because he's miserable. Also, all of his followers are losers—just like Occupy Wall Street, LOL!

Nolte writes:

> "Rises" is a love letter to an imperfect America that in the end always does the right thing. . . . Nolan loves the American people—the wealthy producers who more often than not trickle down their hard-earned winnings, the workaday folks who keep our world turning, a financial system worth saving because it benefits us all, and those everyday warriors who offer their lives for a greater good with every punch of the clock.[5]

And of course, the whole movie was just an excuse by Christopher Nolan to "slap Obama." Press releases from the Southern Poverty Law Center contain more intellectual subtlety and analytical depth.

Nolte's review is exhibit A for the case that the Republican id is driven by the feeling of being right, rich, successful, and in charge regardless of what is actually happening.[6] As Bane said before snapping a capitalist pencil neck, "Do you feel in charge?" Nolte and Shapiro, clueless, would say yes.

New York Times token *faux*-conservative Ross Douthat objected to this reading in a fairly accurate but incomplete analysis.[7] Douthat noted there might be a bit more subtle-

---

[5] http://www.breitbart.com/Big-Hollywood/2012/07/21/Dark-Knight-Rises-Review-Nolte

[6] http://www.counter-currents.com/2012/11/what-makes-republicans-tick/

[7] http://douthat.blogs.nytimes.com/2012/07/23/the-

ty to the question of Gotham's underclass than they are just jerks, but Nolte fired back, doubling down on his, uh, thesis.[8] The bad guys are just "insecure thumbsuckers raging with a sense of entitlement, desperate to justify their own laziness and failure and to flaunt a false sense of superiority through oppression."

"TELL ME ABOUT BANE! WHY DOES HE WEAR THE MASK?"
Where to begin? Perhaps it is best to find some common ground with our misguided and lovably dopey kosher conservative friends. Let's advance the theory that if we both accept the idea of liberal media bias, it is mildly suspicious that biggest blockbuster of the year would be an "ode to traditional capitalism" and a partisan attack on Barack Obama. While contemporary American conservatism's conception of the "Right" has devolved into support of charter schools for blacks and opposing evolution because it's racist, in theory, the Right by definition involves the principled defense of hierarchy. Movie villains that attack egalitarianism, attempt to set themselves up as an authority, or generally have some higher aim besides "chaos" are on the Right, like most of James Bond's supervillains, Loki from *The Avengers*,[9] or the Empire in *Star Wars*.

Therefore, rather than just quoting Republican talking points, it's useful to look at the character of Bane and see how *Big Hollywood*'s charges hold up.

BANE THE NIHILIST
First is the idea that Bane is some sort of nihilist. A nihilist is an individual who doesn't think human existence

---

politics-of-the-dark-knight-rises/
  [8] http://www.breitbart.com/Big-Hollywood/2012/07/23/NY-Times-Rips-Nolte-Dark-Knight-Review
    [9] http://www.counter-currents.com/2012/05/the-avengers/

has objective value or meaning. While Bane could certainly be described as a rather brutal anarcho-primitivist, he certainly does have a belief in actual life versus mere existence. Bane strives for an order worth living in, and ultimately wants justice for all those responsible for the state of society as represented by Gotham.

Bane is motivated to restore the natural balance to the world by putting an end to a decadent society which will inevitably fall. In a sentence: that which is falling must also be pushed. He views Batman as someone who makes things worse by drawing out Gotham's decline and suffering, which is why he must be eliminated. Many of Bane's minions lay down their lives on command to accomplish this ideal, indicative that they believe in something beyond their own personal interests. Their lives are forfeited towards a higher goal, not in a wanton manner *à la* the Joker.

The dialogue spells it out fairly clearly. Bane addresses a henchman as "brother" when he asks him to lay down his life for the mission. "Have we started the fire?" the initiate asks. "Yes," replies Bane. "The fire rises." Unlike the capitalists that Bane exploits to acquire the weapons and equipment he needs to take over the city, Bane is not in it for the money. Staring down at a gaping John Dagget, his former accomplice, Bane pronounces, "I'm Gotham's reckoning, here to end the borrowed time you've all been living on. . . . I'm necessary evil."

Does Bane have a vision of the good beyond just tearing down corruption? Actually he does. Bane possesses a certain reverence for the concept of innocence. In the course of the film it is revealed that Bane was willing to lay down his life to protect the defenseless child Talia. His actions ultimately lead to his own excommunication from the League of Shadows, and a permanent physical impairment. The mask feeds him a painkilling gas that keeps the injuries he sustained at bay. Some of the film's deleted material shows a more primitive version of Bane's apparatus and his training in the League of Shadows under Ra's al Ghul, before he was expelled to keep him away from Ra's al Ghul's daughter.[10] Talia could not forgive her father, until Bruce Wayne murdered him. Only then could Talia and Bane join forces to complete his mission.

This is the heart of Bane's identity, the transformation from a pain-wracked prisoner into an avatar of Justice. As he defeats Batman in single combat, Bane pronounces, "I *am* the League of Shadows. I am here to fulfill Ra's al Ghul's destiny!" Michael Caine's Alfred intones, "His speed, his ferocity, his training! I see the power of belief. I see the League of Shadows resurgent." Say what you will about the tenets of the League of Shadows, Nolte, but at least it's an ethos.

As we recall from the first film, the League of Shadows is a Traditionalist Order dedicated to fighting crime without restrictions from society's "indulgence." Batman is trained by the League, but he turns on them when he is asked to execute a murderer. Incredulous, Ra's al Ghul asks if Bruce Wayne would prefer a trial by "corrupt bureaucrats." Wayne has no response. When Wayne is told that the League plans to destroy the festering rot that is Gotham, Wayne kills many of the League's members and blows up its headquarters. Compared to the League, Wayne/Batman is a liberal.

Incredibly, but perhaps not astonishingly, neither Nolte nor Shapiro *mention* the League of Shadows. It's like trying to explain the transformation of Bruce Wayne into Batman without mentioning the death of his parents. Most importantly, as we find out (spoilers!) at the end of the film, *Bane is not the main villain.* The main villain is

---

[10] http://blogs.indiewire.com/theplaylist/deleted-scene-in-the-dark-knight-rises-explains-banes-origin-movie-becomes-years-no-2-film-so-far-20120807

Talia—Miranda Tate for most of the film—the daughter of Ra's al Ghul who seeks to complete her father's mission. The person who rose from the prison pit was not Bane, but Talia, and it is she who is leading the mission to destroy Gotham. In both the first and third films, Batman is not fighting against chaos, or communism, or high tariff rates, or some other bugaboo of the Beltway *faux*-Right—he's fighting a Traditionalist Order that wants to destroy the city he loves.

The League's justice decrees Gotham should die—Batman's mercy says it should live. Both are fighting for their conception of the good, and willing to die for it. This isn't nihilism, on either side.

BANE THE ECONOMIC SOCIALIST

Bane's attack on the city of Gotham is twofold. First, he attacks the stock market, an action which brings Batman/Bruce Wayne out of retirement. He's confronted by a stock broker who claims, "This is a stock market—there's no money for you to steal." Bane replies, "Really? Then why are you people here?" Bane doesn't take the money—he uses a program to strip Bruce Wayne from control of Wayne Enterprises so he can seize the arsenal and the energy project to build an atomic bomb.

Of course, this is just a means to an end. When John Dagget protests that his company has not been able to absorb Wayne's and claims "I'm in charge," Bane replies calmly, "Do you feel in charge?" Laying his hand lightly on Dagget's shoulder, Bane shows he knows where power comes from—force. When Dagget mutters that he's paid Bane a small fortune, Bane replies, "And this gives you power over me?" "Your money, and infrastructure, have been important, until now." Bane is in service to a cause greater than money—it's not surprising that American conservatives literally cannot comprehend it as coming from the Traditionalist Right.

The real boss of the League, Talia, brings the message home in lines that are delivered early in the movie, but take on a whole new meaning after her true identity is revealed. Speaking to Dagget about a clean energy program, she says, "But you understand only money, and the power you think it buys." We think this is just a champagne socialist looking down on the rich who don't share enough with the poor or spend enough on trendy causes. Actually, the clean energy program is a way to develop a fusion bomb to take control of Gotham, and Talia (who already has control of a vast amount of money) could not care less about Lefty trends. She is also serving the purposes of her father's Order.

The second main attack is against the football game, with Bane blowing up the field after the National Anthem. Nolte's take is "Nolan's love for this country is without qualifiers and symbolized in all its unqualified sincerity in a beautiful young child sweetly singing a complete version of 'The Star Spangled Banner'—just before 'Occupy' attempts to fulfill its horrific vision of what 'equality' really means." Of course, knowing that Bane actually is part of the League of Shadows, we know there's a larger agenda here.

Bane isn't entirely immune to the idea of innocence, as we know how he saved Talia. He even comments while listening to the song, "That's a lovely, lovely voice." Then he says, "Let the games begin!" and pushes the button. The League regards the city of Gotham as hopelessly corrupt and evil, and it's therefore significant that they announce their takeover at a football game—the circus part of bread and circuses. The football game isn't some glorious manifestation of Americana—it's a symbol of how pointless and worthless modern life has become.[11] Bane then announces that Gotham is to rise up and "take back

---

[11] http://www.counter-currents.com/2011/10/big-fan/

their city." The next day, at Blackgate Prison, Bane destroys the myth of Harvey Dent and calls for revolution against the corrupt, who will be cast out "into the cold world that we know, and endure." Gotham, says Bane, will be given "to you, the people."

There's a heavy tone of irony in that last pronouncement, which goes to the heart of Bane's plan. Nolan said that much of the plot was based upon Charles Dickens's *A Tale of Two Cities*, which depicts the moral collapse of Revolutionary France. We know Bane is not a nihilist because of his own pronouncements, actions, and membership in the League. However, has he transformed the League into a vanguard fighter for a socialist commune?

While *Big Hollywood* says yes, there's nothing to suggest that the League of Shadows and its relatively wealthy members and backers (like Talia) are socialists, and they speak consistently of fulfilling, rather than changing, Ra's al Ghul's Traditionalist mission. It's not that Bane is a socialist—it's that he's a Traditionalist who despises capitalism, Revolting Against the Modern World from the Right. American conservatives simply don't get it, trapped into a simplistic worldview where there is Communism on the Left and Capitalism on the Right.

But how do we know this? How can we be sure that we aren't, like *Big Hollywood*, just reading into the movie our own ideological prejudices? Well, it's pretty easy. Bane *directly tells us.*

BANE THE EGALITARIAN REVOLUTIONARY

After "breaking" Batman, Bane takes him to the prison where he lived for years. He tells Bruce Wayne "the truth about despair." There can be no despair without hope, and just as the prison has an opening at the top to drive prisoners mad with the lust for freedom, so Bane will use hope to create greater despair.

Batman is to be punished because he betrayed the

League of Shadows and the cause of true justice. Wayne believed that his "Batman" could be a symbol that lasts beyond him, that anyone could be Batman. As we learned at the end of *The Dark Knight*, Bruce Wayne believes that the people of Gotham are fundamentally good, and that given the choice, they will choose good. Therefore, no matter how bad things get in Gotham, no matter how decadent the elite may be, no matter how much he may personally despise them (even to the point of becoming a recluse), Wayne thinks that which is falling must be propped up. Bane considers this not just mistaken, but despicable. When Batman dismisses the League as a gang of psychopaths, Bane attacks with outraged fury.

Thus, in defeat, Bruce Wayne will be punished by watching Bane torture an entire city. Wayne, after all, lusts for death and release. Bane knows that Wayne's punishment must be more severe, that he has to be *forced* to understand the depth of what he sees as Wayne's evil. Bane will do this by "feeding them [the people of Gotham] hope to poison their souls." Bruce Wayne will watch the people of the city climb over each other "so they can stay in the sun." He will force Wayne to watch as the true nature of Gotham City is unleashed. And then, "when you have understood the depth of your failure, and Gotham is ashes, then you have my permission to die."

Thus, Bane's proto-Occupy speeches aren't about propagating the ideology of the League—it's spiritual poison. He even tells us it's spiritual poison. His screed about giving Gotham back to the people is done to mock the idealism that Batman places in the populace of the city itself. Bane's actions are an attempt to fulfill H. L. Mencken's quip that, "The people get the government they deserve, and they deserve to get it good and hard."

When left to their own devices, the people of Gotham fail miserably at governing themselves. Without the force of Gotham Police Department, the judicial fangs of the

Dent Act, or the confining grip of Arkham Asylum, Gotham quickly falls into disarray. The people of Gotham illustrate that they are nothing more than a mob, who allow psychopaths like Dr. Crane/The Scarecrow judicial power to give people death sentences for pointless reasons. Bane is Gotham's reckoning, not Gotham's executioner. Only the people of Gotham can be the architects of their own destruction.

Bane has zero pretentions about the ability of the people to govern themselves. He gives them every opportunity, and they bring their fate on themselves. The ultimate collapse of Gotham is caused by giving the people the false hope that they are capable of governing themselves through his "revolution." His previous monologue on the worst prison being one with perpetual hope is indicative of this sentiment. He also directly shows Bruce Wayne that his mission in life was a failure. Wayne himself suspects thus, in a dream sequence where the "immortal" Ra's al Ghul tells him that after all of his sacrifices, the most he could accomplish was a lie and that even he must realize Gotham should be destroyed. Subconsciously, even the Batman knows his mission is futile.

There's also one critically important fact that puts the beliefs of the League of Shadows and Bane beyond all doubt—this is a suicide mission. The nuclear bomb that Bane forced Dr. Pavel to build is going to go off after a certain time, regardless of what anyone else says about it. Bane will let Gotham destroy itself, force the rest of the world to see it, and then blow it all up anyway. He'll even sacrifice his life and the life of his men in order to bring about a new beginning on a non-egalitarian foundation. Like Batman, the world will be *forced* to understand.

American "movement conservatism," itself a product of the Enlightenment dogma of infinite human perfectibility, can't cope with this kind of message. Thus, *Big Hollywood* has to ignore the League of Shadows, ignore Talia, ignore the previous films, and even ignore Bane's speech telling the audience *exactly what he is doing* so they can keep on believing in "an imperfect America that in the end always does the right thing." At the Fox News level of cultural analysis, Bane and the League of Shadows develop an intricate, years-long strategy that ends with their own deaths for no other reason than shits and giggles.

THE HERO LIBERAL AMERICA DESERVES?

Needless to say, Batman/Bruce Wayne does save the day. In a sequence heavy with Traditionalist overtones, Wayne climbs out of the pit, is "reborn" as Batman, and defeats the League of Shadows. However, he can't go back. Fulfilling Alfred's wishes for him, he avoids both defeat and death and chooses an anonymous life away from Gotham, away from the society he sacrificed so much to save.

One bit of credit is due the reviewers for comprehending the character arc of Selina Kyle/Catwoman. At the beginning of the film, she claims that she is somehow doing more for the poor than rich philanthropists. She looks forward to the day when "a storm is coming . . . because you're all going to wonder how you thought you could live so large and leave so little for the rest of us." When she actually sees the revolution unleashed, she's disgusted to see how a wealthy family's home has been transformed into squalor. Kyle understands that egalitarianism does not lead to paradise, but horror.

However, ultimately Kyle's actions are motivated by her need to escape. Just like Bruce Wayne, she cannot bring herself to live even in a restored Gotham City. At the end of the film, she's not some happy mama grizzly taking the kids to Mickey D's after a hockey game—she's chosen a wealthy exile with Bruce Wayne. Kyle too is an outsider. Unlike Talia, she chose selfish escape over sacrifice for an ideal.

This is the price of heroism—the hero cannot be part

of the society that he saves. That is why the idea of a superhero can be inherently "fascist"—a superhero is a being of pure will and great power who is held to a different standard so he can impose that will on the larger society. A superhero saves society from itself.

Bruce Wayne comes to this realization reluctantly. After all, the whole point of Batman was that he was supposed to be temporary and that the police and government could take over and function normally once things got to a certain point. This doesn't happen—Robin John Blake is the heir to the title of Batman, having thrown away his own policeman's badge and faith in the system. Like a meat grinder, Gotham will demand more extraordinary men to sacrifice themselves in order to keep functioning. To save the kind of society where everyone is equal, the higher man must allow himself to be consumed as the price of democratic heroism. Democracy can only be saved by people who don't really believe in democracy.

"Do you finally have the courage to do what is necessary?"

Despite the happy ending of Bruce Wayne and Selina Kyle palling around in Florence, the ultimate message of the film, and the trilogy, is far too dark for ever-optimistic American conservatives to internalize. Gotham only functions when it is built on lies. Lacking both an aristocracy capable of leading, and a populace capable of being lead, Gotham reverts to brutal authoritarianism in order to bring about order. This is buttressed by noble lies that would make Leo Strauss blush, and the constant sacrifice of higher men.

The nature of the people themselves ultimately never changes. When left to their own devices, the people allow radical psychopaths to run the roost, a reflection of their own fractured existence. At the end Gotham is saved from total destruction, but once again needs the false lie of a higher man's sacrifice in order to make sense. Bruce Wayne escapes, turns his back on the city, and moves on with his life in a foreign country. Maybe Nolte's charge of nihilism would more accurately apply to the man in the cowl, as opposed to the one in the mask.

Much like modern America though, Gotham can only make sense for so long before the wheels come undone. What is Nolan really saying then? Is it possible he's challenging our notions of what we actually are conserving? Gotham is reminiscent of modern America, decadent, soulless, and lacking any social capital. Is there a Gotham still worth saving? An America? That's Nolan's real question, and something Batman, like conservatives, omit themselves from ever having to answer.

While it is not surprising that *Big Hollywood* and movement conservatism don't "get" the movie, or much of anything else, the reaction speaks volumes about how the Left understands the Right better than the Right understands itself. Conservatives misinterpret the movie because they lack the ability to comprehend anything deeper than corporate profiteering dressed up in platitudes like "free markets" or a "shining city on the hill." Higher ideas like Traditionalism or the nature of man, society, and power might as well be a foreign language to the Last Men pining for the second coming of Ronald Reagan.

Christopher Nolan created a Right-wing film that conservatives are attracted to, but will never truly understand. They can't explain why they like the movie because that requires a new vocabulary drawn from Tradition and the European New Right. Lacking that, we get paeans to the Caped Crusader's fight against clean energy. Still, American conservatives instinctually claim anything with sublimated Right-wing tendencies as their own. All politics is downstream of culture, and unfortunately for conservatives, they lost that battle quite some time ago. However, the impulse for an authentic Right is still there, and the real culture war never truly ends.

Nolan films with a hammer. *The Dark Knight Rises* is a radical traditionalist puncture wound against modernity: not the film we want, but the film we need. Unfortunately, much like Gotham City, the conservative movement and its intellectuals are already too far gone to understand it.

Counter-Currents/*North American New Right*,
December 7, 2012

GOTHAM GUARDIAN:
WILL THE REAL BATMAN PLEASE STAND UP?

JASON REZA JORJANI

Among the neo-pagan American Pantheon of the Justice League, Batman has always had a unique place. He hails neither from a crystalline alien planet of supermen, nor from an equally exotic hidden island utopia. He certainly was not raised in Kansas, like Clark Kent, and he does not work in the hallowed halls of Washington, like Diana Prince. Bruce Wayne is a native son of the grittiest, most powerful, and most corrupt city-state on Earth, *Gotham*—the archetypal image of New York City, a modern Babylon or Rome. He was not endowed by birth with the magical powers of a cryptic super-race that render him virtually invulnerable. His extraordinary abilities are born of long hard training and self-discipline, and many confrontations with an all too palpable mortality. Finally, Batman is not a star-spangled, heaven-sent Apollonian emissary of Truth, Justice, and the American Way. He is of one cloth with the benighted world in the shadows of which he stealthily works. His work often pits him against the authorities as an elusive bane of those who have proclaimed themselves officers of Law and Order. The atmosphere of his world is that of our own—a milieu where the difference between organized crime and legal order is rarely clear, so that even the noblest man must resort to mass deception and terrorism in his thankless task of protecting the decent.

Like any tale that taps into symbols and themes of archetypal power and significance, the Batman mythos has developed a life of its own. In my view, however, its many iterations culminated in the masterpiece trilogy of

Christopher Nolan. During my doctoral studies a Marxist colleague of mine who dressed up as Bane for Halloween claimed that Nolan's "Batman is a fascist." I immediately understood what he meant and replied that he was paying a great compliment to fascism. Perhaps he will think otherwise of Ben Affleck's rendition of Batman, given that the actor's stance on Islam is closer to Bane's than to that of the Dark Knight. The release of *Dawn of Justice* is an opportunity for those of us who have protested that "Ben Affleck is not our Batman" to reflect on the ethos of an *Übermensch* willing to be hated because he is something more than a hero.

When Bruce Wayne, still in his Chinese prison cell, first hears of the League of Shadows from Ducard and dismissively identifies them as vigilantes, Ducard replies: "No, no. A vigilante is a man lost in his quest for gratification. He can be destroyed or locked up. But if you make yourself more than just a man, if you devote yourself to an ideal, and if *they* can't stop you, then you become something else entirely." Later, during the final test in Bruce's training, Ducard says: "You have to become a terrible thought. A wraith. *You have to become an idea!*" What Nolan is referring to here is "Justice" —with a capital J—as a Platonic ideal or idea (Greek *eidos*) above or beyond the plane of transient worldly manifestations.

Christopher Nolan's Batman films sketch out the broad contours of a multi-tiered organized crime syndicate that has effectively become a *de facto* world government. At the *lowest* level are old time mafia bosses like Carmine Falcone and Salvatore Maroni and a variety of new wave gang leaders and drug dealers who each manage their own territories and are grouped in some cases according to race or ethnicity. Lacking any real economic expertise, the first tier of organized criminals must turn to experts in high finance in order to manage their collective investments. Mr. Lau of Hong Kong represents this financier class, and it is significant that he is in turn trying to invest in Wayne Enterprises on their behalf. If a CEO like Earle had still been running Wayne Enterprises, Lau's business deal with the corporation would probably have gone through. While Earle was at the helm of Wayne Enterprises he had departed radically from Thomas Wayne's philanthropic vision for the corporation by becoming involved in heavy arms manufacture, as represented by the microwave emitter chemical agent dispersal unit designed for desert warfare. At the same time, Earle tried to take the company public so as to raise capital from big investors in the arms industry. Bruce ultimately saves his family business from taking this course, but only after Nolan has given us an idea of the second tier of organized crime: *the military-industrial corporation*, which views the first tier of organized criminals as legitimate "no questions asked" investors.

These first two tiers consist of weak-minded people who lack a fearless commitment to principles that they would not violate at any cost. Their ultimate aim is lining their wallets. Most organized criminals hatch their plots to gain something, but this also means that they live in fear of all they have to lose. Both the gangsters and the military-industrial corporatists are glorified thieves. Consequently, more disciplined and intelligent men with well-considered plans and long-term projects find them easy to manipulate. Among this third class of organized criminals are experts in mind control and psychological warfare, such as Dr. Crane (Scarecrow) and his handler Henri Ducard, as well as Ra's al Ghul's daughter and the disciple who was her protector, Bane, and the Islamists that he recruits as his "liberation army."

Crane, an unethical scientist, manipulates the drug dealing activities of the first level of criminals in order to carry out nefarious psychological experiments. Crane is in turn Ducard's pawn. Ducard controls at least part of the international trafficking that brings various illicit substances from Asia to Gotham. Meanwhile, the infrastructure of Gotham has been so badly corrupted that Ducard's men can infiltrate every level of it, to the point of stealthily acquiring classified special weapons designed and manufactured by the military-industrial corporatists. The League of Shadows is not merely after profit. In fact, Bane's rabble-rousing leadership of the Occupy Wall Street movement in *The Dark Knight Rises* demonstrates the essentially anti-capitalist character of the cult. Although it skillfully makes use of mobsters, militarist corporatists, and unethical scientists and technocrats, it is ultimately a cult of "true believers" who reject materialism and creature comforts. That is also what lies behind its thinly-veiled association with radical Islam. This means that even these Assassins can be manipulated. Only the Joker cannot be.

The Joker is not after money, or for that matter any other logically comprehensible advantage or materially definable gain. In *The Dark Knight,* Christopher Nolan shows us this through both Alfred's anecdote about the bandit he chased in the forests of Burma and the Joker's own dramatic decision to burn his half of the laundered money. The former clearly foreshadows the latter. Alfred explains to Bruce that Batman hammered the underworld "to the point of desperation, and in their desperation they turned to a man they didn't fully understand." Bruce then echoes what Ducard said about criminals in *Batman Begins,* namely that: "Criminals aren't complicated." Bruce thinks that they are all after something and they just need to figure out what the Joker wants. Alfred disagrees: "With respect Master Wayne, perhaps this is a man *you* don't fully understand either." He then tells the story about the bandit. Bruce asks Alfred why the bandit would have stolen the stones just to throw them away. Alfred replies: "Well, because he thought it was good sport, because *some* men [Nolan focuses the camera on the Joker's face on TV] aren't looking for anything logical like money. They can't be bought, bullied, reasoned, or negotiated with. Some men just want to watch the world burn." Later, when in the predawn hours Bruce, still half dressed as Batman, is sitting by the window of his apartment overlooking Gotham and contemplating whether he is responsible for Rachel's death, he asks Alfred: "That bandit, in the forest in Burma, did you catch him?" Alfred replies "Yes." Bruce asks "How?" Alfred's ominous response once again references fire: "We burned the forest down."

The two references to the bandit who wanted to watch the world burn and who forces his pursuers to burn a forest down to apprehend him, frame the scene where the Joker sets fire to the money he's extorted from the mobsters and gangsters that he has turned into his playthings. As he burns the mountain of cash the Joker says to one of the gangsters: "All you care about is money, this town deserves a better class of criminal. I'm gonna give it to them. Tell your men they work for me now. This is *my* city." The gangster retorts that his men "won't work for a *freak*," whereupon the Joker delivers one of his most revealing lines in *The Dark Knight*: "Why don't we cut you up and feed you to your pooches. Then we'll find out how loyal everybody really is. Its not about *money*, its about *sending a message: EVERYTHING BURNS!*"

The word "mob" has a dual meaning in Nolan's Batman films. It is not only a reference to the organized crime syndicate that rules Gotham, but also to the masses who allow it to do so. As the Joker recognizes, the people of Gotham are utterly hypocritical. Even though they want law enforcement to hunt down Batman as an outlaw vigilante, and are ready to put him in prison once he turns himself in, they are happy to use him when they really need him. Most of them view him as just as *freak-*

ish and "crazy" as the Joker, and moreover as the catalyst for the "craziness" that has come over Gotham. They share the mob's wish to just go back to the way things were in the old days. Harvey Dent's impassioned plea at the press conference, to the effect that while things are indeed "worse than ever" it is "always darkest just before the dawn" has no effect on them. They do not appreciate him reminding them that although the Batman is an outlaw, the people of Gotham, who have so far been happy to let Batman clean up their streets, are really demanding that he turn himself in because they are scared of a terrorist madman.

The Joker's "social experiment" with the two ferries rigged with explosives is an attempt to demonstrate the validity of his thesis that "when the chips are down, these uh, these 'civilized' people, *they'll eat each other.*" Although this appears to fail, the Joker still makes his point through his "ace in the hole." Both Gordon and Batman agree that the Joker was right to think that if the people of Gotham were to find out what he had turned Harvey into, their spirit would break and they would give up all hope in the good. The only way they can avert this outcome is to cover up the truth that the public cannot handle. This shows that even Harvey Dent's criticism of Democracy is too weak. Recall the exchange between Bruce, his Russian ballerina date, Rachel, and Harvey in a restaurant towards the beginning of *The Dark Knight*:

> NATASCHA (Russian prima ballerina): How could you want to raise children in a city like this.
> BRUCE: Well, I was raised here, I turned out okay.
> DENT: Is Wayne Manor even in the city limits.
> BRUCE: The Palisades, sure. You know, as our new DA you might want to figure out, uh, where your jurisdiction ends.
> NATASCHA: I'm talking about the kind of city that

idolizes a masked vigilante.

DENT: Gotham city is proud of an ordinary citizen standing up for what's right.

NATASCHA: Gotham needs heroes like you, elected officials, not a man who thinks he is above the law.

BRUCE: Exactly, who appointed the Bat Man?

DENT: We did. All of us who stood by and let scum take control of our city.

NATASCHA: But this is a democracy, Harvey.

DENT: When their enemies were at the gates, the Romans would suspend democracy and appoint one man to protect the city, and it wasn't considered an honor, it was considered a public service.

RACHEL: Harvey, the last man that they appointed to protect the Republic was named Caesar, and he never gave up his power.

DENT: Ok, fine. You either die a hero or you live long enough to see yourself become the villain. Look, whoever the Bat Man is he doesn't want to do this for the rest of his life, how could he? Batman is looking for someone to take up his mantle.

NATASCHA: Someone like you, Mr. Dent?

DENT: Maybe, if I'm up to it.

He is *not* up to it, and since both Gordon and Batman agree that Dent is Gotham's finest, it turns out that *no one* is up to it. For most of *The Dark Knight*, Batman believes that Dent is the "real hero" that he "can never be." Bruce sees his own fight against organized crime as provisional, and hopes to be able to create the conditions whereby a public official of a democratic government can take up the struggle through more legitimate means. Rachel clearly influenced Bruce into taking this view. Towards the opening of *Batman Begins* she preaches the virtues of an impartial Justice system over vigilante vengeance, and while Bruce initially responds that "your system is broken" he ultimately tells Ducard that the man he is supposed to execute "should be tried." Ducard replies: "By who? Corrupt bureaucrats? Criminals mock society's laws. You know this better than most." This *was* Bruce's view, but he has come around to seeing things Rachel's way.

Yet in the end we see that Rachel makes excuses to break her promise to Bruce, betraying him to be with Dent—whose character she grossly misjudges as being superior to that of Batman. When Alfred explains to her why Bruce and Dent agree that Batman should not turn himself in, she completely misses the point of what he means by saying that Bruce is not being a hero. She leaves a letter with him whose contents consist of an appalling betrayal of Bruce. Alfred decides to withhold the letter and then ultimately to burn it altogether, which Nolan shows us as one of the montages over Gordon's closing narration in *The Dark Knight*. The juxtaposition of that image together with this narration is intended to suggest that Rachel was just another member of the mob. Bruce blinded himself to her true character (or lack thereof) because without his love for her he would be *so* alone. Alfred burns the letter so that this sudden realization of almost total loneliness will not endanger Batman's compassion for the people of Gotham.

Whether or not Nolan will admit it publicly, one moral of his film is that a Caesar is not only justified under certain circumstances, but that the suspension of democracy need not be temporary. Lucius Fox was mistaken to believe that it is wrong for one man (or a few) to have as much power as the sonar cellular spying system has given Batman, and Bruce Wayne was wrong to think that he had to delegate this power to Fox and then allow him to destroy the machine after only a single use. *The Dark Knight* explores why Democracy is a misguided political system altogether. In this closing narration we see the total inversion of Gordon and Wayne's initial belief that Dent is the true hero and Batman only a temporary stopgap. Dent's heroism is a lie that Batman, who is far more than a hero, decides must be maintained for the citizens' own good. Ra's al Ghul was right that "theatricality *and deception* are powerful weapons," and Batman learns that it is sometimes necessary to use both. Here is the dialogue and narration of *The Dark Knight*'s devastating last scene:

> GORDON: Thank you.
> BATMAN [after having fallen]: You don't have to thank me.
> GORDON: Yes, I do.
> The Joker won. Harvey's prosecution, everything he fought for, undone. Whatever chance you gave us of fixing our city, dies with Harvey's reputation. We bet it all on him. The Joker took the best of us and tore him down. People will lose hope.
> BATMAN: They won't. They must never know what he did.
> GORDON: Five dead. Two of them cops. You can't sweep that up.
> BATMAN: But the Joker cannot win. Gotham needs its true hero [he turns Two Face's head over to the Harvey side]. You either die a hero or you live long enough to see yourself become a villain. I can do those things, because I'm not a hero, unlike Dent. *I* killed those people. That's what I can be.
> GORDON: No, you *can't*, you're *not*.
> BATMAN: I'm whatever Gotham needs me to be.

Call it in.

GORDON [giving a speech before Dent's portrait]: "A hero, not the hero we deserved, but the hero we needed, nothing less than a knight, shining."

[Gordon's closing narration, over images of him breaking down the Bat signal, and the cops chasing Batman . . .]

GORDON: They'll hunt you.

BATMAN: *You'll* hunt me. *You'll* condemn me. Set the dogs on me, because that's what *needs* to happen. Because sometimes Truth isn't good enough [OVER THE IMAGE OF ALFRED BURNING RACHEL'S LETTER], sometimes people deserve more, sometimes people deserve to have their faith rewarded.

GORDON'S SON: Batman. Batman! Why's he running, dad?

GORDON: Because we have to chase him . . .

GORDON'S SON: He didn't do anything wrong.

GORDON: . . . because he's the hero Gotham *deserves*, but not the one it needs right now. So we'll hunt him, because he can take it, because he's not our hero, he's a silent *Guardian*, a watchful protector—a dark knight.

Beautiful, terrible—but only the way a myth, a modern legend can be, right? On the contrary, that is what the mob believes and what the Cosmic Joker who manipulates them wants you to believe. Nolan gives us a hint that he knows otherwise. The card Joker tacks to corpse of the Batman copycat reads: "Will the real Batman please stand up."

In the closing narration of *The Dark Knight*, with its reference to the "guardian" and the noble lie, it becomes clear that Nolan is promoting a new interpretation of the idea of Guardianship that we find in Plato's *Republic*—

the most antidemocratic political text in the history of philosophy. The basic problem of the *Republic* is set forth in the parable of "the Ring of Gyges," from 358a–362b in Book II.[1] This thought experiment is provided as a means to strengthen the argument of Thrasymachus that might makes right, with which *Republic* opens in Book I before going on to counter this view for the rest of the text. Gyges is a Lydian shepherd who, in the midst of a terrible thunderstorm and earthquake, finds the subterranean tomb of a giant in a crevice that has just cracked open the Earth. There are many marvelous things in the tomb, but the giant himself is naked except for a ring, which Gyges removes and slips onto his own finger before leaving the chamber. Later, he discovers that whenever he turns this ring inward he becomes invisible, because others discuss him as if he is not there. He uses this power to have sex with the Queen and murder her husband, installing himself as the King of Lydia.

Plato asks, if there were two such rings, one being given to what we take to be a just man and the other to an unjust man, would not nearly everyone at least privately think of the just man as a fool if he did not go about raping and plundering with impunity, if he did not, in effect, behave exactly as the unjust man does (and would do even more efficaciously with such a ring)? In an annex to the Gyges parable, Plato sharpens the question. Putting aside the ring, what if the state of affairs in the world were such that the man who only seems just in order to profit thereby were to be rewarded for his veiled injustice at every turn, whereas the just man would be taken by the many to be unjust and on that account hunted down and subjected to every variety of torture before in the end being crucified, then who could hon-

---

[1] Allan Bloom, *The Republic of Plato* (Basic Books, Perseus Books Group, 1991), 36–39.

estly say he would prefer to be a just man rather than a man who in the eyes of the many only seems just? Bruce Wayne's extraordinary wealth, honored position as "the prince of Gotham," and his cunning intellect, afford him something like the Ring of Gyges—he could be the seemingly just man, being celebrated as a philanthropist while getting away with all kinds of dastardly deeds or at least living the callow life of a playboy. Instead, he chooses to be a feared, hated, hunted, vigilant guardian who protects those who persecute him and who cannot expect a hero's reward.

The famous or infamous passages on the so-called "philosopher king" as Guardian of the city-state appear from 497b-503b of the *Republic*.[2] I say so-called "philosopher king" because Plato (quite scandalously for his time) thinks that female philosophers are also fit to be Guardians. Three main points are emphasized in these core passages.

The first is that Plato is fully convinced that philosophers cannot quietly retire from politics because they distain its rampant corruption. Philosophers will inevitably be victimized by unjust governments and perhaps martyred. Moreover, given that philosophers who contemplate ideals and are purified through long abiding in a transcendent state, if they turn their efforts to ordering the affairs of the world they would tend to reflect the archetypal patterns within their soul in the re-structured city-state as if in a mirror. In the absence of this, Plato is fully convinced that men of lesser intuition and understanding will always make themselves miserable through bringing about one or another unjust regime as a reflection of their own inner discord. Although the philosopher would rather keep to himself and his peers in a life of quiet contemplation, taken together these two facts

---

[2] Ibid., 176–83.

make it incumbent upon him or her to protect lesser men from their own folly and to temper the violence that these men suffer at each other's hands by taking up statecraft as a public service.

Secondly, to the contrary of the view of those who think that Plato is naively engaging in an idle meander through the land of make-believe, if one reads these passages one finds several times both an insistence that such a regime should actually be implemented and a repeated acknowledgment that although this would be very difficult, and would be vociferously opposed by the mob, it is nonetheless not impossible.

Third and finally, one finds that Plato recognizes that the implementation of such a regime cannot be accomplished through reformist half-measures, but will require a radical revolution that wipes out the prevailing corruption before supplanting it with a more just social order. Like a master craftsman, the Guardian is a "painter of regimes" who will not accept anything less than a blank canvas or "a tablet . . . which, in the first place, they would wipe clean." They "would rub out one thing and draw in another . . . mixing and blending . . . ingredients" for a new "image of man."

Needless to say such a revolution will be resisted by the mob who are incapable of understanding that it is for their own good, and that even those of them who are killed in the course of it will benefit by being reincarnated into a more just society. Therefore, a certain measure of deception will be necessary in order for the Guardians to forward their noble-minded project. This is the aspect of the doctrine of Guardianship in the *Republic* that is most evidently alluded to in Nolan's use of the Batman mythos to critique democracy. In the course of the *Republic*, Plato offers us two principal examples of the role that a "noble lie" might play in establishing a just social order.

The concept is introduced at the core of the so-called 'myth of the metals' recounted from 413a–417b, with the key passage being at 414c: "Could we . . . somehow contrive one of those lies that come into being in case of need, of which we were just now speaking, some one noble lie to persuade, in the best case, even the rulers, but if not them, the rest of the city?"³ The second reference comes at 457a–462c in the context of proposals as to how to coerce compliance with controversial eugenics and population control policies, with this striking pronouncement as its fulcrum at 459d: "It's likely that our rulers will have to use a throng of lies and deceptions for the benefit of the ruled. And, of course, we said that everything of this sort is useful as a form of remedy."⁴

The content of these noble lies might not seem to have much in common with the noble lie that Batman decides to have Commissioner Gordon tell the people of Gotham, but their form is the same. In all cases, the noble lie is really about using deception or trickery as a way to fool people into becoming something that they would not otherwise have been capable of becoming. It is a way of crossing over and redefining the boundaries of the possible, like pretending to hold a child who is just learning to tread water in the deep end of the pool but holding him so lightly that he is already really keeping himself afloat but would still drown if he were made aware of this. Or, in a more sinister example, it is like forcing people you want to protect to face a false enemy so that they will build their strength in earnest and be more prepared for a real enemy that you know will arrive later.

The message of Hermes, the Trickster, may bring new boundaries decreed by Heaven, but only because he already crossed the old ones or brought people to cross

---

³ Ibid., 93.
⁴ Ibid., 138.

them.⁵ He is the god of the threshold.⁶ Although he upsets the established social order, Hermes is most decidedly *not* the god of democracy; he will align himself with any number of different (and even opposed) political systems for strategic reasons.⁷ He is known to play both sides, perhaps to provoke them into a *generative* strife. It appears that the Hermes archetype is not only at work in the Joker, but also in the response that the Joker's apparent victory elicits from the Dark Knight. In fact, the Batman and the Joker are an alchemical conjunction of opposites with tremendous transformative potential. A majority of Gothamites and most of the police force want to go back to a time before Batman, and the city's organized criminals think that the "craziness" the Joker has unleashed is just too much. Yet, as Alfred explains to Bruce, he "crossed the line first," and as the Joker explains to Batman, "there is no going back." Hermes has crossed the boundaries and calls forth a new order out of Chaos.

A good student of Plato recognizes that "do not unto others as you would not want others to do unto you" is a principle as necessary for maintaining the cohesion of a gang of criminals as it is for governing a city-state. It is based on the lowest common denominator of self-interest, not on any contemplation of a moral ideal. Furthermore, it falsely assumes that most people are able to make a contract of their own free will, and to recognize each other as equal partners in such a contract.

When Batman decides that he must tell a Platonic noble lie, when he realizes that his proper role is as a republican Guardian and not as the hero of a democracy sustained through a social contract, something of the

---

⁵ Lewis Hyde, *Trickster Makes This World: Mischief, Myth, and Art* (New York: Farrar, Straus and Giroux, 2010), 7.
⁶ Ibid., 7–8.
⁷ Ibid., 215.

Trickster's dynamism has transformatively insinuated itself into his character as well. To recognize this, in the compelling context of Nolan's films, is to better discern the esoteric Hermetic dimension of the Platonic project. Truth lies beyond the limits of the possible, such that the instauration of Justice makes impossible demands of allegedly "conservative" but unprincipled hypocrites. "You must be joking," they say—to which the only answer is for the real Batman to stand up.

SUPERHEROES, SOVEREIGNTY, & THE DEEP STATE

GREG JOHNSON

The superhero genre in comics and movies was largely created by Jews.[1] In some of my writings on film, I have argued that superheroes largely function as symbolic proxies for Jews.[2] Superheroes, like Jews, are outsiders and "freaks." They are, moreover, immensely powerful outsiders. Thus, lest they incite the fear and ire of their host populations, they must practice crypsis to blend in.

Superheroes also play an apologetic role for Jewry. Despite near total Jewish hegemony in the media and educational system, the public mind is still aware of stories of secret Jewish cabals plotting to harm the *goyim*, from the Elders of Zion to the Project for a New American Century and the Office of Special Plans. Thus, to immunize the public from automatically regarding such cabals with suspicion, the superhero genre portrays these immensely powerful and secretive outsiders—individually, and in groups like the Justice League, the X-

---

[1] See Ted Sallis' review of *From Krakow to Krypton: Jews & Comic Books*, http://www.counter-currents.com/2011/10/from-krakow-to-krypton-jews-and-comic-books/

[2] See my reviews of *Hellboy* and *Hellboy II: The Golden Army* in *Trevor Lynch's White Nationalist Guide to the Movies*, ed. Greg Johnson, Foreword by Kevin MacDonald (San Francisco: Counter-Currents, 2012) and *Man of Steel* in *Son of Trevor Lynch's White Nationalist Guide to the Movies*, ed. Greg Johnson (San Francisco: Counter-Currents, 2015).

Men, and the Avengers—as committed to the morality of egalitarian humanism and benevolently serving the interests of humanity.

Of course, in reality the Bolsheviks, neocons, and their like more closely resemble supervillains than superheroes. Thus, to inoculate the public mind from drawing that sort of conclusion, supervillains are usually portrayed as Nazis, or symbolic proxies for Nazis. Basically, supervillains are illiberal, elitist, and nationalistic, with traditional or archaic rather than modern values, whereas superheroes are liberal, globalist, and devoted to serving their inferiors.

But superheroes can exemplify Right-wing political themes as well. I want to argue that superheroes are the fictional genre that best illustrates Carl Schmitt's antiliberal concept of sovereignty. Specifically, I wish to speak about the masked vigilante genre, epitomized by Batman, in which accomplished but still biologically human individuals use criminal methods—including masks and disguises—in the pursuit of justice. I am less interested in superhuman aliens and mutants, although they too can function as vigilantes. And I am not talking at all about superheroes who simply rescue people in peril, which is legal in any system. I am talking about superheroes who take the law into their own hands, who break the law in order to do justice.

Masked vigilantes are staples of literature and legend, including Robin Hood and the Sicilian Vendicatori and Beati Paoli, all from the middle ages. But the most well-attested historical examples of masked vigilantes are, of course, the Ku Klux Klan.

Batman breaks the law in order to save the law, when the legal system encounters an opponent that it cannot master. There is a moving scene in Christopher Nolan's *The Dark Knight Rises* in which Commissioner Gordon explains why he turned to Batman, a vigilante, for help:

There's a point, far out there, when all the structures fail you, and the rules aren't weapons anymore, they're . . . shackles, letting the bad guy get ahead. One day . . . you may face such a moment of crisis. And in that moment, I hope you have a friend like I did, to plunge their hands into the filth so that you can keep yours clean!

This is a perfect description of the function of the sovereign as described by Schmitt. Sovereignty means supreme political authority within a territory, as opposed to political subjection. Within a society, the sovereign is the ruler, as opposed to the ruled. A sovereign nation rules itself, as opposed to being ruled by others. But what is the essential characteristic of the sovereign? In *Political Theology*, his short book on the concept of sovereignty, Schmitt states that: "Sovereign is he who decides on the exception."[3]

To understand what is exceptional, one needs to understand what is normal. In human affairs, the normal is what usually happens. Normal circumstances can, therefore, be anticipated by legislators, and the laws they create can be enforced by functionaries—police, bureaucrats, judges, etc.—in a simple "deductive" way: If a particular event falls under a general law, justice requires a certain prescribed course of action.

But as Aristotle pointed out, in human affairs, generalizations pertain "not always but for the most part," meaning that there are not just normal circumstances but also exceptional ones. But exceptional circumstances—if they really are exceptional—cannot be anticipated by legislators. Thus merely applying the existing laws in

---

[3] Carl Schmitt, *Political Theology: Four Chapters on the Concept of Sovereignty*, trans. George Schwab (Cambridge, Mass.: MIT Press, 1988), p. 5.

exceptional circumstances cannot produce just results.

Justice, therefore, requires not just following rules in normal circumstances but also exercising discretion in exceptional ones. This act of discretion has two aspects: discerning *that* we are facing an exception and discerning *what* we must do to cope with it.[4]

Such discretion can exist on all levels of the legal system. Cops on the beat, judges in courthouses, and bureaucrats in offices all have to discern the just path in exceptional circumstances. Of course the discretion of ordinary policemen, judges, and bureaucrats can be reviewed and overruled by higher-ups in the hierarchy.

But you can't appeal and second-guess forever. Eventually, you will come to a final arbiter, the final decider. The same is true of legislative or judicial deliberation. At some point deliberation has to end. Matters must be decided. Questions must be closed so that we can act.

The supreme law in any system is the constitution. And when the constitution encounters an exceptional situation, there must be a supreme decider: he who de-

---

[4] I argue that this discretion presupposes a *prior, intuitive* knowledge of justice, of the right thing to do. We cannot conclude that following a given law produces an unjust outcome in exceptional circumstances unless we have *another* access to justice besides the law itself. Since this knowledge is not articulated in rules, I call it an *intuitive* awareness of justice. This intuitive knowledge has to exist *prior* to our attempts to articulate what justice is. Only because we *already* intuitively know what justice is can we judge general laws to be inadequate to exceptional circumstances. This same intuitive sense of justice also allows us to discern the just course in unique circumstances. Intuition furnishes a non-universal "law" to guide us. Plato's arguments about justice in the *Republic* all depend on this prior, intuitive knowledge of what justice is. In the *Nicomachean Ethics*, Aristotle called this intuitive grasp of justice "equity" (*epieikeia*).

cides *that* society is facing an exception, and he who decides *what* to do about the exception. This is the sovereign as Schmitt defines him. He is the supreme power, uniting judicial, legislative, and executive functions.

Now a vigilante or superhero does not literally become a sovereign—unless, of course, he pulls off a *coup d'état*. But he performs the *function* of the sovereign by deciding that he faces an exceptional situation and what he must do to fix it. Beyond that, he takes full responsibility for his acts, since all he can appeal to is his own judgment of right and wrong. But unlike a true sovereign, who is honored for serving the common good, the vigilante knows he will be punished. But he is willing to bear the sacrifice.

Many societies make provisions to give individuals plenary powers in emergency circumstances. For instance, in normal circumstances, the Romans like the Spartans divided the executive power. The Spartans had two kings and the Romans had two consuls, each consul being accompanied by 12 lictors carrying the fasces, the emblems of political authority.

However, in emergency situations, the Romans would appoint a dictator, who was accompanied by 24 lictors, symbolizing the unification of executive power. Emergency situations included fighting wars and quelling insurrections, as well as presiding over religious rituals and civic elections. When necessary, Roman dictators could ignore or break the normal law with impunity. But dictators were appointed only for the duration of the special situation or for a fixed period, after which they surrendered their powers.

Another example of a provision for emergency plenary powers is Article 48 of the Weimar German constitution, which allowed the chancellor to assume dictatorial powers in an emergency. Adolf Hitler appealed to Article 48 to assume dictatorial powers after the Reichstag arson.

Those who defend the thesis that "Hitler did nothing wrong" will be pleased to learn that he became dictator in a completely legal manner.

In Christopher Nolan's *The Dark Knight*, prosecutor Harvey Dent defends Batman's vigilantism by likening it to the role of the Roman dictator: "When their enemies were at the gates, the Romans would suspend democracy and appoint one man to protect the city. It wasn't considered an honor; it was considered a public service." Of course there is an important difference: the Roman dictator was a legal office, whereas Batman is an outlaw. Nevertheless, Bruce Wayne sees Dent as someone who might make Batman unnecessary by performing his functions *within* the legal system.

But that is not really possible, for Gotham is a liberal democracy. One of the basic principles of liberal democracy is "government by laws, not men." Liberals see human decision ("arbitrariness") as a source of injustice, which must be eliminated from the political system. From Schmitt's point of view, however, one cannot eliminate decision from politics. One's only choice is to own up to it, to take responsibility for decision, and to make sure that the best possible people are empowered to decide—or, like liberals, we can try to evade that responsibility.

The liberal idea of government is a machine that runs by impersonal rules to make sure that everyone is treated justly and fairly, but which is indifferent to the quality of the individuals who compose society and the cultivation of virtue. If decision is inevitable, then we have to find and shape the best possible deciders. But if society can simply operate like a machine, human vice and mediocrity are no impediments to good government.

Liberals also believe that if they just put the right procedural rules in place, they do not need to worry about the consequences of acting according to those rules.

Thus they are dismissive of political philosophies that depend upon any vision of the future, any notion of a common good or ideal society that we should strive for. You can argue all you like that liberal principles lead to catastrophic consequences—for instance, free trade undermines national sovereignty and First World living standards; the free movement of peoples leads to social alienation, miscegenation, and conflict; or expressive individualism leads to cultural degeneracy, collapsing families, and personal unhappiness—but liberals simply deny that consequences have any moral weight. Instead, they will cling to their procedural notions of the good—their sacred "principles"—even though the world might perish.

Liberalism seeks to evade decision in all aspects of politics. But the fundamental pathology of liberalism is the evasion of specifically *sovereign* decision, which forces the sovereign function outside the law. Those who would save liberalism from itself, when it fails to meet the challenge of the exception, must sacrifice themselves by becoming outlaws. In Commissioner Gordon's terms, they must "plunge their hands into the filth" of illegality so that public officials like him can keep their hands "clean." Clean according to the laws that are "shackles" rather than "tools" of justice. Clean of "arbitrariness," clean of the responsibility of deciding, clean of sovereignty.

Schmitt teaches us that sovereignty ultimately reposes in men, not laws. This is true even in liberal systems, which refuse to admit it openly. Which just means that liberal democracies are ruled by *secret* sovereigns, men who exercise decision as they hide behind the laws and pretend that their hands are tied, that they are just following orders, that their hands and their consciences are clean.

In liberal society, there are two kinds of secret sovereigns. First, there are the founders, the framers of the constitutional order who *decided* what the fundamental laws will be. As I put it elsewhere:

> Laws are ultimately created by decisions. Thus those who believe that decisions must always be governed by laws are simply abandoning their own freedom and responsibility and choosing to be ruled by the free decisions of those who came before them. Just as the deist model of the universe depends upon divine wisdom to frame its laws and set the machine in motion, liberals depend on the human wisdom of the Founders who created the constitution.[5]

This is why Americans revere the Founders and recoil with horror at the thought of another Constitutional Convention. The founders made fundamental decisions so we don't have to, fundamental decisions that we fear to make. The Founders were great men, and we are lesser ones. The Founders, of course, were not the products of the system they created. But we are.

Second, because the founders of a liberal system cannot anticipate every exceptional circumstance, sovereignty must be exercised in the present day as well. And if no legal provisions are made to give plenary powers to a sovereign in a time of crisis, that means that sovereignty must be exercised outside the law.

This leads us to the concept of the "deep state," which, as far as I know, is the only Turkish contribution to political thought. The idea of the deep state (*derin devlet*) is a coinage of Turkish Islamists. It refers to a shadowy network concentrated in the Turkish military

---

[5] http://www.counter-currents.com/2014/08/schmitt-sovereignty-and-the-deep-state/

and security services which spreads throughout the bureaucracy and judiciary and intersects with organized crime. The deep state works to maintain Turkey as a secular, nationalist society, primarily working against Islamists, Left-wing radicals, and Kurdish separatists, all of whom threaten the Kemalist order. The Deep State is behind at least four Turkish military coups. The failure of the July 2016 coup has given Recip Erdogan the pretext for purging the deep state from Turkish institutions. Time will tell if he has succeeded.

The concept of the deep state needs to be distinguished from other extralegal forces that influence political policy. It is easy to confuse the deep state with such notions as an "establishment," a permanent bureaucracy, secret agencies, smoke-filled rooms, lobbies and pressure groups, political "inner parties," NGOs, and even secret initiatic societies, all of which shape political policy and negotiate between interest groups.

These groups are simply part of politics as usual. Thus in Schmittian terms, they have nothing to do with *sovereignty*, which comes to light only when politics as usual breaks down. The deep state is where sovereignty resides if a system fails to legally institutionalize it. The deep state consists of people who have real power within a given system and who work together, killing or dying if necessary, to preserve the system when it enters a crisis. In James Cameron's 1994 movie *True Lies*, Arnold Schwarzenegger works for a secret US government organization called the Omega Sector. It is named "omega" because it is the system's "last line of defense." That is the function of the deep state.

I believe that the American fascination with superheroes, conspiracy theories, and secret societies feeds upon an awareness that liberal democracy punts on the question of sovereignty. We know that our government is riddled with shadowy networks working to advance special interests at the expense of the body politic. And we desperately hope that at least one of these groups might actually be looking out for the system in a time of crisis.

Since White Nationalists wish to create a new political system in North America, and since we are hoping to be helped by crises in the present system, it behooves us to ask who would kill or die to preserve the American system in such a crisis. Is there an American deep state? If so, where does it lie? If not, where might it emerge?

The military is the most likely place where a deep state would emerge, since soldiers take oaths of loyalty more seriously than politicians and are prepared to kill and die for the present system. But a fatal crisis might include catastrophic military failure. It might involve a standoff between the military and other institutions that can only be resolved by outside parties. In such cases, Bonapartism would no longer be an option.

I don't think that the organized Jewish community would function as a deep state in a crisis. As I argue in another essay:

> Organized Jewry is the most powerful force in America today. In terms of politics as usual, Jews get their way in all matters that concern them. But although organized Jewry surely would intersect with an American sovereign deep state, if America faced a severe constitutional crisis, I do not think that Jews would step in to exercise the sovereign decision-making functions necessary to preserve the system. They would surely try to stave off a crisis for as long as possible, to preserve their wealth and power. Then they would try to milk a crisis for all it is worth. But ultimately, I do not think they would risk their own blood and treasure to *preserve* the American system, for the simple reason that the Jews *today* show no sign of caring about

America's long-term viability. It's not their country, and they act like it. They are just using it, and using it up. They are not stewarding it for future generations. Therefore, they will not take responsibility for its preservation. In a real crisis, I think their deepest instinct would be simply to decamp to friendlier climes.[6]

The sovereign combines ultimate power with ultimate responsibility. Like the captain who goes down with his ship, he knows that the price of failure is death. Jews want wealth and power without responsibility. They'll shrug off dishonor rather than suffer death. They're survivors. Thus, in the end, Jews are just toying with and merchandising the idea of superheroes who constitute deep states and play the sovereign role. But that does not stop White Nationalists from taking the idea seriously and planning accordingly.

First, no matter where an American deep state might emerge, the difference between a true White Nationalist and a mere racially-conscious conservative is that we regard the system's ultimate guardians as our worst enemies. Our goal is not to save this system but to create a new one, which makes us revolutionaries, not conservatives.

And that makes us a different kind of outlaw than Batman, who like so many patriotic and public-spirited white people today, accepts the egalitarian-humanist ethos and thus sacrifices himself to preserve a system rigged to destroy him. We want to create a new system, rigged to encourage our survival and flourishing, not our degradation and destruction.

Second, if White Nationalists are serious about creat-

---

[6] http://www.counter-currents.com/2014/08/schmitt-sovereignty-and-the-deep-state/

ing sovereign white homelands, we need to think of ourselves as a government in exile, as the guiding intelligence and deep state of a stateless people. Just as the British opposition parties maintain shadow cabinets, we must form a shadow government. A League of Shadows, if you like.[7] Every regime is founded by an elite. Every regime is governed by an elite. Every regime turns to an elite in a time of crisis. So let us become that elite. In a world without sovereign white homelands, we must create them. In a world without superheroes, we must become them.

Counter-Currents/*North American New Right*,
July 27, 2016

---

[7] There are many examples of such shadow governments, but the one that fits best with the theme of superhero as sovereign vigilante is Operation Nemesis, the secret organization of Armenian exiles formed in Boston in 1920 to assassinate the Turkish architects of the Armenian Genocide, which they proceeded to do, almost to a man. See my review of Eric Bogosian's *Operation Nemesis*, http://www.counter-currents.com/2015/07/operation-nemesis/

CAESAR WITHOUT GODS:
CHRISTOPHER NOLAN'S DARK KNIGHT TRILOGY

CHRISTOPHER PANKHURST

Christopher Nolan's Dark Knight Trilogy (*Batman Begins*, *The Dark Knight*, and *The Dark Knight Rises*) begins with the evocation of fear which becomes the motivational impulse for Bruce Wayne's story. As a child he accidentally falls down a disused well, and, whilst he lies trapped and injured, he is terrified by a flock of bats that appear like a chthonic force of nature from the bowels of the earth. His father rescues him and tries to encourage a sense of self-overcoming: "Why do we fall? So we can learn to pick ourselves up." The entire trajectory of the three films is set in motion with this brief motivational dictum.

When the young Bruce attends a performance of the opera *Mefistofele* with his parents he experiences a panic attack brought on by some of the performers dressed as bats. Their appearance causes his primal fear to re-emerge. The family cut short the opera and leave, and this is why his parents end up being shot by a mugger in a street outside the theater.

Some years later Bruce attends a parole hearing for his parents' murderer. He takes a gun intending to kill the man on his release thus resolving both his sense of fear and his guilt at his parents' deaths. Unfortunately (or fortunately) for Bruce, the freed man is first shot by one of mob boss Carmine Falcone's employees as a punishment for testifying against Falcone. Bruce then seeks to run away from both his inheritance and his unresolved inner conflicts, ending up in a foreign prison where he meets Ra's al Ghul (under a false name) from the League of Shadows. At the culmination of his training with the

League, Bruce learns that they intend to destroy Gotham. In fact, the League presents itself as a group of Spenglerian shock troops who, throughout history, have repeatedly intervened at the end point of a civilization, pushing it over the edge to destruction in order to allow something new and vital to come into existence:

> This is not how man was supposed to live. The League of Shadows has been a check against human corruption for thousands of years. We sacked Rome; loaded trade ships with plague rats; burned London to the ground. Every time a civilization reaches the pinnacle of its decadence, we return to restore the balance.

In this encounter with Ra's al Ghul, Bruce learns to become a strong, superempowered individual, but he is also presented with the opportunity to ally himself with a particular view of historical unfolding. The League exists to oversee the trajectory of civilizational development and to ensure that at the end point of a civilization there is a complete destruction of the decadent forces. As far as the League is concerned, Gotham represents the pinnacle of decadence, and as Gotham is modeled on New York this is perhaps not entirely surprising. Once Bruce Wayne learns of the League's strategic goals he rejects them and decides to oppose them. But, apart from the training he has undergone with the League, he does take one important lesson from them. Ra's al Ghul forces Bruce to confront his personal demons (and, perhaps significantly, Ra's al Ghul's name is Arabic for 'head of the demon'):

> To conquer fear, you must become fear. You must bask in the fear of other men. And men fear most what they cannot see. You have to become a terrible thought. A wraith. You have to become an idea!

But the purpose of such a transformation is clear:

> A vigilante is just a man lost in the scramble for his own gratification. He can be destroyed, or locked up. But if you make yourself more than just a man, if you devote yourself to an ideal, and if they can't stop you, then you become something else entirely . . . A legend, Mr. Wayne.

This is the crucial point in Bruce Wayne's (and the film's) development. Bruce has an opportunity to embrace an ethos that transcends, not only the self, but also the limitations of a late civilization. But such a prospect is intensely problematic for Bruce Wayne. As the head of Wayne Industries, he is not a typical inhabitant of Gotham; he is in some ways an aristocratic figure, almost a sort of medieval prince. This is partly suggested by the appearance of Wayne Manor which is meant to resemble an English stately home (and in fact, for both the original and the reconstructed Wayne Manors, English stately homes were used). And the point is further emphasized by casting the English actor Sir Michael Caine in the role of Alfred. Even more significantly, Bruce Wayne's name is embedded in the architecture of Gotham. The central landmark of Gotham is Wayne Tower, and the transport network around the city is provided by Wayne Industries. The hub and spokes of the city are nominally identified with Wayne, and he is born into a sense of *noblesse oblige* due to his father's dual bequest of wealth and social responsibility. One of Bruce Wayne's roles in this film is to return as the head of Wayne Industries and thus fulfill his inheritance and reclaim the name of the father.

Thus, Bruce chooses to reject the meta-historical role offered to him by the League of Shadows and to instead focus on a very personal project of self-overcoming. He is offered Spengler, but he accepts Jung.

C. G. Jung's concept of individuation is an important theme throughout the trilogy. It is first introduced by the rogue psychiatrist Dr. Jonathan Crane whose alter ego is Scarecrow. Whilst in the persona of Scarecrow, Crane drives Falcone to madness with his fear toxin, and Falcone is left babbling the single word, "scarecrow." Crane explains that, "Patients suffering delusional episodes often focus their paranoia on an external tormentor, usually one conforming to Jungian archetypes . . . in this case a scarecrow." It is significant that the film introduces this concept as a false explanation by a criminal psychiatrist.

At the end of *Batman Begins*, Bruce has defeated Ra's al Ghul, he has appropriated the symbol of the bat to represent the overcoming of his own fears, and he has forged an effective alliance with Jim Gordon of the Gotham police force. The crime syndicates have begun to be defeated, and corruption has been tackled. But the appearance of the Joker's calling card at the end of the film gives an intimation that not all is well. It also establishes that Bruce Wayne and Gordon are engaged in a process of endlessly deferring the collapse rather than preventing it, a tacit admission that the League of Shadows represents an inevitable process rather than a mortal adversary.

When the Joker does appear in *The Dark Knight* he enables Bruce to confront the shadow side of his self. According to Jung, the shadow sometimes appears in the form of the trickster, a mythological motif that has both a collective, social function as well as an individual one. This makes sense because, as already mentioned, Bruce is nominally identified with the infrastructure of Gotham.

The Joker represents the trickster in a number of ways. The trickster is the embodiment of the unconscious; he is not evil, it is just that his distance from any sense of rational order makes him do appalling things. Alfred recognizes this when he says that, "some men aren't looking for anything logical, like money. They can't be bought, bullied, reasoned, or negotiated with. Some men just want to watch the world burn." The trickster can also appear as either male or female, just as the Joker does when he cross-dresses as a nurse. Even his observation that, "I'm a dog chasing cars. I wouldn't know what to do with one if I caught it! You know, I just . . . do things," hints at the theriomorphic form that the trickster will sometimes adopt.

But most significant, and most sinister, is the Joker's lack of a biography. When he is arrested the police are able to find no trace of him on their files, and they discover that his clothes are all hand made. He is disturbing because he appears to have no relational ties with society. He even seems to have no name. The subtextual implication here is that identity cannot exist without some form of societal context. The Joker emerges *ex nihilo* and has no connection to anything. Consequently, his motivations, as such, can never be comprehended because they can never be located in a particular context. He is a shade who is not afraid of death because, effectively having no identity, he is already dead.

He also makes up stories about his past, giving contradictory accounts of how he got his facial scars. This lack of a biography lends an ethereal chill to the characterization. In contrast to a book such as *The Killing Joke*, which explores the family background and origin story of the Joker, *The Dark Knight* turns him into someone who seems to have never existed in society at all. We simply can't get a grip on him because he doesn't exist as a social agent. Whereas Bruce Wayne is unusual in the extent to which his own interests are embodied in the infrastructure of society, the Joker is unique because he has absolutely no interface with society at all. No family, no branded clothing, no police record; nothing. This makes him a particularly powerful iteration of the Joker because more mythic qualities are allowed to speak through him.

Meanwhile, Batman has been becoming more and

more identified with the role of a Caesar figure. This is made explicit in the discussion between Bruce, Rachel, and Harvey Dent:

> **HARVEY DENT**: When their enemies were at the gates, the Romans would suspend democracy and appoint one man to protect the city. It wasn't considered an honor, it was considered a public service.
>
> **RACHEL DAWES**: Harvey, the last man who they appointed to protect the Republic was named Caesar, and he never gave up his power.

This identification of Batman with Caesar is only an intensification of the already existing identification of Bruce with Gotham. Just as Bruce seems to embody the interests of Gotham due to his investment in its infrastructure, the Dark Knight emerges as the Caesar figure who embodies the state in his own person. And this makes explicit the notion that the late phase of a civilization is the propitious moment for a Caesar figure to appear. There is thus a progression from Bruce Wayne in his role as technocrat ruler of the city state, the *de facto* prince of Gotham, to the Dark Knight who becomes Caesar as a desperate response to the declining power of the state.

As the Dark Knight progressively becomes closer to a Messiah figure, the importance of the Joker's role as the shadow in the guise of the trickster becomes more apparent. In an essay on the trickster, Jung writes:

> Only out of disaster can the longing for the savior arise—in other words the recognition and unavoidable integration of the shadow creates such a harrowing situation that nobody but a savior can undo

the tangled web of fate."[1]

In both a personal and civilizational sense this can be seen to be particularly true for the film. The two figures are linked in such a way that the emergence of the Dark Knight as Caesar must necessarily coincide with the appearance of the Joker as the trickster. They respectively represent the response to and the background disorder of the late phase of a civilization. This is why the Joker insists, "I think you and I are destined to do this forever."

Something worth noting is that although the trilogy is filled with gestures towards religious notions, there really are no religion and no gods anywhere to be found in Gotham. In Spengler's terms, this accords with the *formlessness* of the age of Caesarism. The prior animating spirit has now disappeared from the civilization. The age of money has coarsened and promoted cynicism to such an extent that the very possibility of a religious awakening seems risible. But one real joy of Nolan's trilogy is the way in which he continually allows the *form* of prior religious functions to intrude into the secular world of Gotham. Whether this is in the form of the Dark Knight as a Messiah figure, or the apparent immortality of Ra's al Ghul when he reappears in *The Dark Knight Rises* as an actual wraith, there is an implicit acknowledgement that the forms of religious observance are ineradicable, even if the gods themselves are not.

In *The Dark Knight Rises*, the League of Shadows reappears in the guise of Bane. There is little to be said here about the course of this film other than to note that the League's reappearance serves to underscore the inevitability of the form of historical unfolding that they describe.

---

[1] C. G. Jung, *Four Archetypes*, vol. 9, Part 1 of the *Collected Works of C. G. Jung* (Princeton: Princeton University Press, 1970), 151.

The Dark Knight has committed himself to preventing their victory, but the trilogy seems resigned to its inevitability. This is what gives a real feeling of tragedy to the films.

The ending of *The Dark Knight Rises* seems problematic. After recovering the nuclear bomb from Ra's al Ghul's daughter, Batman flies off out to sea where the bomb detonates. It would appear that, having once more deferred the process of civilizational decline, the Dark Knight has now completed his mission of personal transformation in an act of supreme self-sacrifice, laying down his life to save his people. His realization of Messiah status is complete; perhaps there will also be a cult that will develop around him allowing the citizens of Gotham to rediscover the sense of the numinous that has now become so obscure to them.

But we quickly learn that the Dark Knight's sacrifice is actually no such thing. At the end of the film, Alfred sees Bruce and Selina Kyle seated at a nearby table whilst on holiday in Florence. Apparently, Batman did not die in the explosion after all. John Blake, the police officer who earlier confronted Bruce about his social responsibilities, then discovers the Batcave, and we are led to believe that he will adopt the persona of Robin and continue the fight against corruption in Gotham.

There is a school of thought that interprets Alfred's discovery of Bruce and Selina as a dream, or fantasy, although the film itself makes it pretty clear that Bruce had set up his faked death in advance. Still, the happy ending does seem out of keeping with the darkness that had preceded it. There is something unsatisfying in learning that Bruce has emigrated to a life of domestic happiness, leaving the fight to save Gotham up to someone else. Thinking about the ending along these lines reveals that, in fact, the "happy" ending merely masks a very deep pessimism. The decline of Gotham will continue with increasingly ineffective interventions from the forces of law and order. Bruce's personal transformation, which might have achieved its apotheosis in a moment of true self-sacrifice, has been put aside for the purpose of domestic tranquility. And the possibility of Gotham's renewal through an act of numinous immolation is shown to be predicated on a lie.

According to Spengler, the age of Caesarism represents the closing of a chapter in history. With no more room for spiritual development, the civilization becomes a personal plaything of various rulers who no longer express the numinous vitality felt directly in the early and high stages of its development:

> By the term "Caesarism" I mean that kind of government which, irrespective of any constitutional formulation that it may have, is in its inward self a return to thorough formlessness. It does not matter that Augustus in Rome, and Huang Ti in China, Amasis in Egypt and Alp Arslan in Baghdad disguised their position under antique forms. The spirit of these forms was dead, and so all institutions, however carefully maintained, were thenceforth destitute of all meaning and weight. Real importance centered in the wholly personal power exercised by the Caesar, or by anybody else capable of exercising it in his place.[2]

Hence the inevitability of Bruce's very personal quest and the impossibility of his grasping the truths uttered by Ra's al Ghul, truths which are literally above time. Bruce is living at the wrong point in history to be able to engage in a mission that might enable a transcendence of the self and the realization of a truly aeonic role, so he must con-

---

[2] Oswald Spengler, *The Decline of the West* (New York: The Modern Library, 1962), 378.

front his own inner demons and meanwhile do what he can for Gotham. True history cannot take place here.

The full pessimism of the trilogy's message can be seen with this passage from Spengler:

> With the formed state having finished its course, high history also lays itself down weary to sleep. Man becomes a plant again, adhering to the soil, dumb and enduring. The timeless village and the "eternal" peasant reappear, begetting children and burying seed in Mother Earth—a busy, easily contented swarm, over which the tempest of soldier-emperors passingly blows.[3]

With his retirement from Gotham and his new life of family and contentment, Bruce reveals the full force of the trilogy's pessimistic view of history. Gotham continues to fall, hope is built on a falsehood, and each victory over the forces of chaos is brief. In Bruce Wayne Gotham really does get the hero it deserves.

Counter-Currents/North American New Right,
July 19, 2016

---

[3] Ibid., 381.

A Dark Knight
Without a King

Will Windsor

Christopher Nolan's Batman Trilogy deserves its large audience among White Nationalists. *Batman Begins, The Dark Knight,* and *The Dark Knight Rises* all comprise a canon in the superhero genre that stands above the rest, perhaps only exceeded by *Watchmen* in its representation of Right-wing themes and philosophy. Much has been said about the emphatically Right-wing character of Batman's villains, especially the League of Shadows, but less has been said about the Rightist aspects of Batman himself.

Typical of the superhero genre, Nolan's Batman protects the liberal system. Batman is nominally portrayed as the defender of liberalism, a "heroic" savior of the neoliberal, cosmopolitan city of Gotham. He ostensibly believes in the democratic system and its institutions that are worth fighting for. All it needs is a little help from a crime-fighting billionaire. In this, Nolan's Batman is no different from other superheroes, who follow the same narrative pattern of protecting the existing system as its hero from the villain who critiques the system and seeks to destroy it.

Yet in Nolan's trilogy, this narrative framework is routinely undermined and revealed as a weakness in Batman's character. A tragic flaw that serves as the habitual source of Batman's undoing and frustration. Furthermore, unlike conventional superheroes who are portrayed as "heroic" because they champion liberal values, Batman betrays the system he seeks to uphold, acting outside of the rule of law in defiance of liberal notions of justice. Indeed, once the mask is removed from Batman as the "silent guardian, watchful protector" of neoliberalism, a much deeper Right-wing character emerges.

Symbolism & Imagery

The first clue that Batman is a Right-wing character are his appellations the Dark Knight and the Caped Crusader. Both refer to medieval European warriors who adhered to an ethical code glorifying honor, righteousness, and loyalty. Such men are reviled by the Left as exemplified in Obama's equation of crusaders to present-day jihadists. Other medieval allusions are woven into Batman's backstory. Bruce Wayne's family is Gotham nobility, they built most of Gotham, and are its most wealthy and powerful family, emblematic of American-style aristocracy. When Bruce Wayne's parents are shot by a vagrant in *Batman Begins*, they had been attending an opera, a hallmark of aristocratic culture. As sole heir of the Wayne family, Bruce is free to engage in higher pursuits as he is secure in his wealth and power like most feudal elites. The mob boss Falcone even refers to him as the "prince of Gotham" when Bruce confronts him about the release of his parent's killer in *Batman Begins*. As such, Batman can be viewed as a contemporary version of a noble who transforms himself into a crime-fighting knight, both of which are representative of historical institutions on the Right.

Notwithstanding his use of advanced military technology, Batman fights with a grittiness that is not flashy or enhanced by any supernatural capabilities; it's authentic and brutal. He fights with his fists and defeats his opponents through mastery of an ancient style of martial arts, one that employs the psychological (deception and fear) as well as the physical (strength and technique) to overcome enemies. The art of combat, a celebration of *virtus*, is unequivocally Right-wing and plays a prominent role in the Batman character. Altogether, the aesthetics of Batman harken to pre-liberal masculinity, when men were nobles and knights, fought for their people, believed in grand visions, and pursued higher callings in life. Even the uninitiated receive a healthy dose of manliness, the bedrock of any Right-wing movement.

All of this is set against the backdrop of Gotham, a giant metropolis that amalgamates America's premier globalist cities: New York, LA, and Chicago. These shining liberal utopias are accurately depicted in Gotham. Crime and corruption are rampant, choking off the city's lifeblood. The streets of Gotham are dark, dreary, and deadly, bereft of all beauty and awash in the refuse of humanity that liberalism produces but cannot eliminate. Gotham is the future that awaits our Western cities. Even the rich in Gotham are not safe, something we have yet to look forward to in the coming years. Within this dying liberal dystopia springs forth Batman, entrenched in medieval symbolism and masculinity, bringing real change: righteous violence.

ACTIONS

The most Right-wing aspect of Batman is his fascist use of force. Batman recognizes that order must be brought about by violence. Violence is necessary; violence is justice. The Left believes that "violence is not the answer," that criminality and corruption can be solved by displays of acceptance and understanding, or programs that address the "root cause" of such problems. Batman understands that only violence can stop criminality. No social programs will ever stop the criminal dregs of society from becoming who they are. Batman flouts the legal system's procedures that protect criminals, and defies society's laws that restrain law enforcement. The actions of Batman reveal the failure of "the rule of law," which requires a vigilante to break the law in order to uphold the law. Society's preoccupation with the rights of criminals has disarmed authority from the ability to properly fight criminality. Justice requires force. Batman exemplifies this truth.

We on the Right understand that force in itself is amoral. Its morality depends on who wields it and who triumphs. Liberalism restricts the use of force and violence against criminals because it sympathizes with the criminals, the miscreants, and the reprobates that liberals see as victims of an oppressive white society. Libertarians fear the potential abuse from more violence. On the Right, however, we understand that violence cannot be avoided. It is necessary to maintain civilization. The goal is to find those worthy of the power, those of higher character and justice, those like Batman. This can only be achieved in a society that appreciates violence and virtue, not one of democracy and equality.

In Nolan's trilogy, the villains reinforce the conclusion that Batman's use of force is just and that he should use more force not less. In *The Dark Knight*, Batman deploys a city-wide wiretapping device to finally locate the Joker despite the liberal objections of Lucius Fox who sees it as violation of sacred privacy rights. Batman is proven correct in his fascist use of force as it successfully results in the Joker's location and capture, demonstrating the value of force when used for the right purpose. Earlier in the movie, the necessity of uninhibited force is again justified when Batman travels to China and kidnaps Lau, the mob money launderer, and brings him back to Gotham for trial. The law had become not only a shield but an enabler of criminality as Lau exploited the law's limits on jurisdiction and extradition to advance his criminal empire. Only through force unbound by the law does Batman render justice against Lau.

In this respect, Batman pays heed to Ra's al Ghul's counsel in *Batman Begins* that "criminals mock society's laws." The irony is that Ra's al Ghul delivered this pronouncement in light of the need to kill extrajudicially, which serves as the final test for Bruce Wayne to become a member of the League of Shadows and "demonstrate his commitment to justice." In the Nietzschean figure of Ra's al Ghul, the killing of the condemned by the righteous is the ultimate expression of justice. Bruce Wayne objects to such a test, asserting that the execution of a murderer should only be delivered by a court of law. Wayne's refusal to kill is arbitrary. Although Wayne recognizes the necessity of being freed from legal limitations, he quixotically believes that killing alone requires judicial sanction—the demarcating line between just avenger and unjust vigilante. In Snyder's rendition of the character in *Batman v Superman*, Batman's refusal to kill is rightly done away with. However, Nolan uses the refusal as a critical mistake.

The Joker lays bare Batman's "self-righteousness" as utterly foolish, and exploits it just as Ra's al Ghul warned: "Your compassion is a weakness your enemies will not share." The Joker willingly allows himself to be captured by Batman knowing that he will be taken into custody unharmed. Once inside the interrogation room, the Joker delivers his punch line that both Harvey Dent and Rachel Dawes have been kidnapped and bound in separate warehouses, and Batman must choose which one to save before they are both blown up. Batman chooses Rachel but inadvertently saves Harvey, as the Joker lied about their locations. Rachel dies, and Batman loses his closest friend and love interest. He also fails to "save" Harvey Dent who turns into the madman Two-Face in the aftermath. If Batman had simply executed the Joker earlier when he had the chance, such a loss would have been avoided, but sadly he lacked the "courage to do what is necessary" to defeat evil.

Worldview

Another dimension to Batman's character worth examining is his worldview. The killing of his parents motivates Wayne to transform himself into a crime-fighting superhero to clean up the streets of Gotham. Initially, he is consumed by rage after the release of his parents' killer and embarks on a seven-year journey of criminality in an attempt to make sense of a corrupt world. His crimes land him in a Chinese prison where he is rescued by the League of Shadows, a Traditionalist order that trains Bruce to become a member. Under Ra's al Ghul's tutelage, he learns to sublimate his rage towards the higher cause of justice and vengeance. Although Wayne objects to their radical vision, the League of Shadows imparts to Wayne a warrior ethos that animates his actions.

Bruce fights to uphold liberal institutions, but his actions and motivations derive not from his belief in egalitarian morality but rather from a warrior code that is one-part League of Shadows and one-part his own moralistic fabrication. The net result is a warrior code that recalls the spirit of chivalry: protecting the weak, fighting injustice, defending the city. But is also deeply flawed as it perpetuates a corrupt system. Understood in this light, Batman fights for Gotham not because he believes in egalitarian ideals, but because he wants to defeat criminality, the source he perceives as the cause of his parents' deaths.

This rejection of equality is openly hinted at in *The Dark Knight* when Batman impersonators question Batman's supremacy as sole vigilante: "What gives you the right? What's the difference between you and me?" to which Batman dismissively responds "I'm not wearing hockey pads." Bruce Wayne also mocks the lifestyle of our cosmopolitan elites by relying on an outwardly hedonist image of Bruce Wayne who spends his time lavishly drinking and consorting with bimbos as the perfect cover to avoid suspicion in a society that glorifies such vanities as normal. Batman does fight for the system and not against it, but he stands apart from the system, motivated instead by a warrior ethos unbound by society's rules that make his actions admirable but ultimately frustrating. Ra's al Ghul diagnoses such a warrior ethos that fails to do "what is necessary to defeat evil" as a weakness derived from the denial of the Will. In a scene that appears inspired by Nietzsche, Ra's al Ghul instructs Wayne on the primacy the Will as they spar on a frozen lake:

> RA'S AL GHUL: Your parents' death was not your fault.
> [Bruce attacks Ra's al Ghul with his sword]
> RA'S AL GHUL: It was your father's.
> [Bruce furiously attacks Ra's al Ghul, but is easily defeated]
> RA'S AL GHUL: Anger does not change the fact that your father failed to act.
> BRUCE WAYNE: The man had a gun!
> RA'S AL GHUL: Would that stop you?
> BRUCE WAYNE: I've had training!
> RA'S AL GHUL: The training is nothing! The will is everything!
> [Ra's al Ghul bests Bruce once again]
> RA'S AL GHUL: The will to act.

This Nietzschean Will is constantly denied and suppressed by Batman. His failure of the Will is ultimately the most important Right-wing critique offered in Nolan's films, most strikingly the disasters that follow when Batman captures the Joker instead of executing him. A knight's moral code of chivalry serves little good for the protection of a system that rejects all the values a chivalric code was meant to uphold. In the end, Batman's worldview is self-defeating. Wayne can never save Gotham because the corrupt system never changes. Wayne refuses to "become who you are"—the prince of Gotham, its ruler—and instead believes that lesser men like Harvey

Dent should govern the city. A knight can fight against the forces of corruption, but only a king can change the system to end corruption and injustice.

VILLAINS

Batman's denial of the will makes his character rigid. His belief in Gotham's institutions denies the heroic nature within him that his villains attempt to bring out.

The Joker taunts Batman to release the inner beast, to free himself entirely from society's norms, as the Joker has done. He points out that society already considers Batman a freak like him, so why bother following their rules. "The only sensible way to live in this world is without rules" the Joker says, to live according to one's Will, to be authentic. Western man has subjugated our Dionysian self to Apollo, always making sure that actions proceed from a reasoned plan, which the Joker delights in destroying. A little chaos is needed to reignite tribal man; he's just ahead of the curve.

Similarly, the villain Two-Face who starts out as Harvey Dent, envies Batman's power. He instructs Bruce Wayne on how the Romans would suspend democracy and appoint an absolute ruler during war, which was considered an honor for the man chosen. Harvey in a sense wishes to be Batman, to take control of the city by force, whereas as Batman would rather be Harvey Dent, who attempts to change society through the system. Two-Face implores Batman to be Gotham's hero, but Batman shirks from such power. The juxtaposition, as with the Joker, is an explicit call for Batman to use more force, to take control of his city.

The villains Bane and Ra's al Ghul of the League of Shadows challenge the very identity of Batman as just and morally good. Both villains rail against Batman's desire to save Gotham. Batman is not justice but injustice. Gotham must die. It must be destroyed so that it can be reborn anew, cleansed of its decadence. The only justice that can be rendered is Gotham's reckoning, and by standing in the way, Batman is unjust. In *Batman Begins*, Wayne describes his vision for Batman as an incorruptible symbol of hope, to inspire people that "good" will win out. In *The Dark Knight Rises*, Bane ridicules Batman as worse than an empty symbol, a symbol of despair:

> There's a reason why this prison is the worst hell on earth . . . Hope. I learned that there can be no true despair without hope. So, as I terrorize Gotham, I will feed its people hope to poison their souls. I will let them believe they can survive so that you can watch them clamoring over each other to stay in the sun.

Bane is directly challenging Batman's sole purpose and declaring him not a symbol of justice but of self-delusion and despair. Justice rests upon truth, but Batman would rather perpetuate a lie that Harvey Dent was Gotham's white knight than tell the truth about his murders because "people will lose hope." In contrast, Bane's whole message is about truth, the harsh truth about Gotham as a lost city of decadence and corruption that must be eliminated. Bane reveals the truth about Harvey Dent to the people: "You have been supplied with a false idol to stop you from tearing down this corrupt city." Batman is thus shown to be a deceiver standing in the way of truth and justice. The League of Shadows show Batman for what he is: a fruitless charade that merely prolongs the decay. Rather than wait out the decay as civilization crumbles, Bane and the League of Shadows accelerate "progress," allowing democracy to be fully realized by handing over the rule of the city entirely to the people. "Gotham is yours. None shall interfere. Do as you please," Bane tells the denizens of Gotham, releasing the masses to consume themselves and tear apart the city as its final destiny.

This is why Batman's villains are far more memorable and interesting than Batman himself. They are free to pursue their will, whereas Wayne is trapped in a fool's game where nothing materially changes, one that the Joker finds irresistibly amusing: "You won't kill me out of some misplaced sense of self-righteousness. And I won't kill you because you're just too much fun. I think you and I are destined to do this forever."

Conclusion

While recovering in Bane's prison pit, Batman hallucinates a vision of Ra's al Ghul. It is a subconscious admission of his failure:

> You yourself fought the decadence of Gotham for years with all your strength, all your resources, all your moral authority, and the only victory you achieved was a lie. Now you understand Gotham is beyond saving and must be allowed to die.

Even though Wayne rises from the pit to save Gotham one last time, he knows Ra's al Ghul is right and that he has failed. He can't let Gotham be destroyed on his watch, so he performs his final deed and then passes the buck to somebody else and leaves the city for good. Wayne is destined for heroic nobility, but he is insincere. He does not remain true to his calling of justice, failing to do what he knows to be right and necessary out of misplaced self-righteousness. He lacks the will to act, the will to power. Maybe one day a truly heroic Batman will emerge, one that uses his superhero abilities to rule the people not serve them.

Nonetheless, Batman conveys an altogether Right-wing impression that can be admired and appreciated for its traditionalist outlook and approach. The medieval symbolism and imagery, as well as the depiction of righteous violence all invoke important Right-wing attributes concerning masculinity, discipline, and order. Where Batman falters, his villains are there to offer compelling foils and to shed light on the right path to take. The Nolan Trilogy offers a total work of art dedicated to a fascist superhero in need of his King. In the coming ethnostate, we can look forward to a Batman who finds him.

Counter-Currents/*North American New Right*,
August 4, 2016

THE PONDEROUS WEIGHT OF THE DARK KNIGHT

JAMES J. O'MEARA

Reviewers of the new Batman movie, *The Dark Knight Rises*, on various Alt-Right sites have been reasonably led to ask why comic books—excuse me, "graphic novels"—have come to dominate Hollywood. Since both industries were founded by and are dominated by You Know Who, the answer seems easy—ethnic networking—why pay royalties to the *goyim*?

There is, as usual, a deeper reason, and, as usual, you're gonna get it here!

By deeper I mean this: the ethnic networking is obvious (at least, to those of us who can See); we need to know why it works, why it succeeds, and why so well, and why just now.

Clearly the real problem is not Them but rather the state of the world—the cosmic cycle—that makes Them able to function with extreme prejudice.

In some worlds, the cream rises to the top. In other worlds, what rises is the scum. In a material world, the most materialistic prosper. And who is more materialistic, less intellectual or spiritual, than . . . Them?

As I was looking for something else, this rather untypical passage caught my eye in René Guénon's *The Crisis of the Modern World*:

> In such a world there is no longer any room for intellectuality or for what is of a purely inward nature, for those are things which can neither be seen nor touched, weighed nor counted; there is only

room for outward action in all its forms, including those most completely devoid of meaning. Furthermore *it is not surprising that the Anglo-Saxon passion for "sport" gains more and more ground every day; the ideal of the modern world is the "human animal" who has developed his muscular strength to the utmost; its heroes are the athletes, should they even be brutes; it is they who awaken the popular enthusiasm and it is their exploits that command the passionate interest of the crowd*; a world in which such things are possible has indeed sunk low and would seem to be nearing its end. ("A Material Civilization"[1])

What does this have to do with the Rise of the Dark Comic?

We need a still finer-grained analysis. The rising tide of scum has not lifted all comics. Superman, above all, is still treated as an impossible figure of fake "nobility" and "goodness," a sort of lumbering Golem, an embarrassing leftover of the Cold War. We still mock George Reeves' pot-bellied, baggy suited TV image, and if not for his tragic accident, Christopher Reeve would no doubt have long since entered an Adam West or William Shatner stage of profitable self-mockery, especially after the last, disastrous, self-directed series entry.[2]

The popular figures, Iron Man, Spider Man, and of

---

[1] http://www.worldwisdom.com/public/viewpdf/default.aspx?article-title=A_Material_Civilization_by_Rene_Guenon.pdf

[2] Actually, George Reeves' decline into drink, drugs, gigoloism and a still unexplained death, would seem even more tragic than Reeves, but only interests TV conspiracy cultists. "His life was filled with hard-drinking men, manipulative women, mafiosos and a career that plummeted like a comet." See Sam Kashner's *Hollywood Kryptonite: The Bulldog, the Lady, and the Death of Superman* (New York: St. Martins, 1997).

course, Batman, are usually distinguished from Superman as being "flawed" or "troubled"—supposedly another sign of Their "psychologizing" influence—but I'd rather focus on the more basic fact: whatever their "problems," they are, unlike the "invulnerable" Superman, just like you and me—only slightly better.

On this front, I think it would be useful to compare the two leading movie "franchises": Batman and James Bond (also subject to a recent reboot, complete with an ethnic-OK actor).

During the initial James Bond phenom, Kingsley Amis wrote an excellent study, *The James Bond Dossier*, a splendid example of the kind of valuable results one can get from paying serious attention to "mere" pop culture, blurring the line between "fan boy" and "literary critic."[3]

Amis makes the valuable point that Bond, like all successful fantasy figures, is never too far from what we can comfortably imagine ourselves to be, especially if we "could only get the right break."

Bond, obviously has no "super powers," other than a certain amount of intelligence, physique, and good, albeit "cruel," looks. What he accomplishes is due to extensive training, the latest equipment, and a good tailor. All of which is lovingly described as part of Fleming's characteristic label fetishism, allowing us to imagine our closets and resumes loaded with just the right gear.

Amis calls attention to a very sly and subtle line in which Bond is described as being, of course, "the best shot in the service" . . . other than his instructor.

And we could be too, with just a bit of imagination, and a cracking good instructor, and a snooty British armorer to steer us away from buying "a woman's gun."

Before taking on Hugo Drax at cards, Bond bones up

---

[3] Kingsley Amis, *The James Bond Dossier* (London: Jonathan Cape, 1965).

on cheating methods—books on card sharping seem to make up the bulk of his small home library[4]—and as for his legendary drinking and smoking, when you add it all up—and Amis, bless him, does just that—it's not really more than we could do with a little effort, thus earning the comfortable feeling of being a bit of a rogue but without headaches, pink elephants, and emphysema.

Even so, by *Thunderball* Bond is so worn out that the service sends him to a health spa! Hard work, but great benefits—a dream job indeed! And of course, while there he engages in what publishers would call "a deadly game of cat and mouse" with an Italian count, and uncovers an anti-NATO plot—just like we would!

I'm reminded of a more recent phenom, when Madonna was still put forward as some kind of icon of muscular femininity—hard to recall, now that she seems more like your drunk aunt dancing with her dress over her head at the wedding—and defensive women would retort, sure, I could look like that if I had no job, a private, state-of-the art gym, and a staff of personal trainers.

It's all a question of degree, of course—Peter Parker's radioactive spider bite is only a little less implausible than Kryptonian birth, while Tony Stark's Iron Man is

---

[4] Like his *lumpen*-audience, Bond doesn't fancy books. His fans get the hint: Jack Kennedy established his George W. *faux*-regular guy cred by letting on that he enjoyed Fleming, and thus brought the Bond boom to the States. Kennedy was the prototype of the type analyzed here: a physical wreck kept together with drugs and braces who promoted an image of "youth" and "vigor" while pursuing disastrous 007-style ventures in Cuba and Vietnam. Don Draper shows his disdain for his snooty French father-in-law by displaying a Bond book on his bedside table, just like Jack showed those Frogs how to do things in Indochina. The season ends with Draper, deserter and fake, having a drink while the jukebox plays "You Only Live Twice."

Bond finally deciding he's not going to return the equipment "from the field" and will just keep it, thank you very much, Q.

But of them all, it's Bruce Wayne who has it in spades. If we inherited a gazillion dollars, a vast mansion, an industrial concern that manufactures advanced weaponry and armor; oh, and a faithful retainer that just happens to be ex-SAS—essentially, the Old Bond played by David Niven in the first, comedic *Casino Royale*—then we too could be the Dark Knight.

As Jack Nicholson's Joker says, "Where does he get all those wonderful toys!"

Similarly, the late Paul Fussell points out in his invaluable study *Class: A Guide Through the American Status System* (New York: Touchstone, 1992) that the popularity of *The Official Preppy Handbook* (despite the title, another product of Them) was a result of insinuating that a certain level of class, the upper-middle or lower-upper, could be had, or at least simulated, which to the American is just as good, by simply buying the right items, and if the houses and cars were out of reach, you could always buy the shirts and shoes, with the stores and labels conveniently listed, Fleming fashion.

And thus Ralph Lipshitz of the Bronx was reborn as Ralph Lauren of Southampton.

No surprise when the recent, failed, attempt at a reboot, *True Prep: It's a Whole New Old World* (New York: Knopf, 2010), proclaimed the King and Queen of Prep to be . . . Barrack and Michelle Obama. Of course! Fantasy fulfilled! Now Michelle can feel proud to be an American.[5]

---

[5] Similarly, the Hannibal Lechter saga, post the middlebrow reboot *The Silence of the Lambs*, postulates a criminal super-genius who dotes on Florence, everyone's favorite tourist stop, and eventually escapes to become . . . a minor Floren-

As figures of average man fantasy, it's no surprise that both Bond and Bats put their lives and even sanity on the line in the defense of modern capitalism and democracy, even while openly disdained for their efforts. (Bond, for example, becomes obsessed with Blofeld both as a world-conspirator and the killer of Bond's wife, and eventually winds up with amnesia in a Japanese fishing village, then brainwashed by SMERSH and sent to kill M.)

Bond's Britain, as Amis documents, is the pre-War world of Raffles and Sapper, already disappearing when Fleming was writing, while modern film Bond confronts a female M that regards him as a perhaps useful but still dangerous anachronism.

Batman opposes the "weaponized Traditionalism" of the League of Shadows, and does so in the name of the most characteristic feature of the Reign of Quantity: democracy, "a few good people," and other notions with nothing to recommend them other than the "common sense" idea that more people weigh more, and therefore count for more. I mean, what else could determine policy, or truth? And yet, he is a hunted vigilante, living in exile, the scapegoat of all of Gotham's problems.

But these are just the slight inconsistencies of heroic fantasies designed for the unheroic masses of an antiheroic world.

But where do Guénon's remarks about "sport" and "the human animal" come in? I think the popularity of Batman, and what makes him a more modern, popular and relevant figure than even Bond—despite Daniel Craig's heroic

---

tine museum official. Oh, but the shopping! Like any American middle-brow, he seems to spend his time drinking espresso in quaint cafes and communicates with Agent Starling via fancy perfumes from chic boutiques. In the happy ending of *TDKR*, Bruce Wayne fulfills Lechter's ultimate fantasy: brunch in Florence with Agent Starling.

attempts at rebooting the Bond franchise—comes from a related development: the Schwarzenegger factor.

Alan Helms in *Young Man from the Provinces*,[6] his account of his career as "the most celebrated young man in all of gay New York" in the 1950s, discusses his aversion for exercise and the gym, and notes that in some 3000 years of painting and sculpture of the Ideal Male Form, not once did anyone come up with something looking like Arnold Schwarzenegger.

Until, as Guénon might have added, now.

We've mentioned the laughable figure of Superman, poor George Reeves who had to take his brown costume (picks up better in black and white) home each day to wash and iron, slowly shrinking over the course of filming the series until the sleeves came up to his midforearm. "Family Guy" mocks Robert Mitchum as an "out-of-shape in-shape '50s guy" (easy to do if you're a cartoon, buddy). *Mystery Science Theater* chuckles at actors who "look like a 19th-century 'strong man.'"

Standards, in short, for actors have tightened up, if you will, and imagination—and suspension of disbelief—are apparently too "purely inward," as Guénon would say, to be operative. Ignoring the lessons of Henry James, we childishly demand "the real thing."

Of course, no actor can be "perfect" and, along with the parallel demand for "state of the art" special effects—another rich source of mockery on MST3K—we see the reason for what will be, ultimately, the complete replacement of actors and sets by CGI. And, like Madonna, no one except an unemployed maniac is going to hit the gym to grunt their way to perfect Arnoldhood. (Hmm, actually quite a few around these days . . . .)

---

[6] Alan Helms, *Young Man from the Provinces: A Gay Life Before Stonewall* (Minneapolis: University of Minnesota Press, 2003).

What to do in the meantime? Where is the plausible fantasy of the Average Man who worships over-developed brutes but is too lazy to pump iron? Enter the Batman. Or rather, the Bat Suit.

As the protagonist in *Money*, a mid-'80s novel by Amis' son Martin, wearily admits, "I need a full-body cap."

The post-graphic novel Batman has been played with more or less controversy by a series of rather unprepossessing actors, typical of "modern men" such as Michael Keaton—fresh from success as "Mr. Mom"—or the decidedly wispy, rather metrosexual Val Kilmer and Christian Bale. It's as if behind the mask of the Dark Knight was—Alan Alda.

Correspondingly, the costume has changed from Adam West's drab TV-wrestler's garb to ever more state of the art armor and fake musculature—rather like the mighty American football players with their space-age padding, versus supposedly "girly" soccer players who make do with T-shirts and shorts.

The more "everyman" inside the suit, the more "superman" the suit itself.

The exception of course was the Schumacher-directed George Clooney film. Although not spectacularly muscular, Clooney was far too much of an alpha male to "fuel the fantasy," and while the new bat-and-robin suits were mocked as "homoerotic" the real problem was not that as such, but rather the related notion of calling attention to the body as such, with the suits' thrusting codpieces, lovingly delineated buttocks, and even sculpted nipples.

Again, the more powerful the man inside, the less the suit needs to compensate. And that, in case you ever wondered, was why Batgirl's suit was sans nipple. As Jodie Foster says on the commentary track to *Silence of the Lambs*, Agent Starling doesn't need a "woman suit" like Buffalo Bill to be powerful, since she is already a real woman.

The crowd wants seedy, alcoholic Tony Stark, played by seedy, drug-and-alcohol ravaged Robert Downey, in the Iron Man suit, not lithe, handsome and well-endowed David Bowie in his Goblin King leotard.

Perhaps to compensate, look, it's Schwarzenegger as Mr. Freeze, and get a load of that suit!

And speaking of Arnold's suits: the "business suit" was designed with the same purpose: weedy London business men, deprived of the invigorating benefits of outdoor labor, could still project a masculine silhouette. Contra snippy critics of the '80s, the padded, "power suit" was invented in the 1800s, and for men, not women.

Thus, as Fussell points out, Schwarzenegger looks even more ridiculous in a suit, no matter how "well-tailored." Even Fussell couldn't imagine Arnold becoming a governor.[7]

Conversely, we see, contemporaneous with new Batman films, the suit employed as a weapon in *Mad Men*. To drive the point home, in an early episode, we see Don Draper serenely glide out of the pot-smoke filled apartment of last night's bimbo, beatniks and cops grabbing some tenement wall to make way for the Man in the Suit.

How appropriate then that the League of Shadows should announce itself by attacking a sporting event, and be able to take out Gotham's "top" officials by blasting them out of their skybox.[8]

---

[7] Nor his own son, Samuel, becoming a bodybuilder: S. W. Fussell, *Muscle: Confessions of an Unlikely Bodybuilder* (New York: Poseidon Press, 1991).

[8] Paul Kersey, who has tirelessly documented the role of pro and college sports in creating an alternate reality of PC-approved "human animals," observes "There's a reason Bane started his "revolution" in the movie *The Dark Knight Rises* at a football game."
http://stuffblackpeopledontlike.blogspot.com/2012/07/blog-post.html

And was there any doubt that the pumped-up, barechested Bane would, in the end, be defeated by the Man in the Bat Suit and his wonderful toys?

Counter-Currents/*North American New Right*
July 28, 2012

MAN OF STEEL

TREVOR LYNCH

I have never liked the character of Superman. He is not a man who has transcended humanity toward something higher. He is simply an alien, who looks like one of us, and who comes equipped with a whole array of superpowers. From a Nietzschean and Faustian standpoint, that translates to zero appeal. I am not interested in being rescued by a superior being. I am interested in *becoming* a superior being. Furthermore, none of the Superman movies or TV shows ever managed to make this character compelling to me (although I love the John Williams score for Richard Donner's 1978 film).

But when I went to see *Man of Steel*, I was prepared to be sold, for this movie is a team-up of two of Hollywood's leading young *goy* geniuses: director Zack Snyder (*Watchmen*) and Christopher Nolan, director of the Dark Knight Trilogy and *Inception*, who co-wrote the script with long-time Jewish collaborator David Goyer.

But *Man of Steel* is a deeply disappointing movie. Compared to *Watchmen* and the Dark Knight Trilogy, which are intellectually and emotionally deep, complex, and involving, *Man of Steel* is pretty much a brainless, soulless spectacle.

The underlying problem seems to be that Snyder and Nolan just aren't that crazy about the character of Superman either. Hence they have delivered an uninspired, by-the-numbers, would-be "Summer Blockbuster." (Aren't blockbusters also a kind of bomb?) *Man of Steel* even stoops to the last refuge of bad scripts: the movie is swarming with cameos. ("Look, it's Kevin Costner!" "Look, it's Morpheus!" "Look, it's that wog from *Battlestar Galac-*

tica!") After this film and *Sucker Punch*, it is time to put Zack Snyder on artistic probation. *Watchmen* may have been just a fluke. This whole movie reeks of cynicism and greed.

But there is also a deeper, older stench underneath. As I have argued in my reviews of *Hellboy* and *Hellboy II: The Golden Army*,[1] comic-book superheroes largely function as symbolic proxies for Jews, who virtually created the genre. Superheroes, like Jews, are always outsiders and "freaks." They are, moreover, immensely powerful outsiders who must engage in crypsis to blend in, lest they incite the fear and ire of their host populations.

The superhero genre also plays an indispensable *apologetic* role for Jewry. For in the case of superheroes, these immensely powerful and secretive aliens are benevolently disposed to their host populations, magnanimously enduring the fears and suspicions of their narrow-minded and xenophobic inferiors whose interests they serve out of a commitment to the morality of egalitarian humanism.

Jews, of course, use their superpowers and knack for crypsis to rather different ends, ceaselessly scourging the *goyim* with plagues like Bolshevism, free market capitalism, feminism, multiculturalism, pornography, psychoanalysis, non-white immigration, Zionism, endless wars, and, to top it all off, the ongoing genocide of the white race.

This, of course, is supervillain behavior, but the superhero genre inoculates us from drawing that conclusion by making supervillains into perpetual Nazis, or symbolic proxies for Nazis and other nationalistic, anti-egalitarian, xenophobic, and traditional-minded whites (but never nationalistic, anti-egalitarian, xenophobic, traditional-minded Jews).

---

[1] In *Trevor Lynch's White Nationalist Guide to the Movies*.

Superman is, of course, one of the most explicitly Jewish superheroes. Superman was created in 1933 by two Ashkenazi Jews, Jerry Siegel and Joe Shuster, and from the beginning he was cast as an "American" antipode to the German "supermen" who rose to power in 1933. Like Moses, Superman was set adrift in an ark and found and adopted by an alien family. Superman's original name is Kal-El, and his father was named Jor-El, "El" being a Hebrew word for "God" and a root of such names as Israel and Elizabeth.

In *Man of Steel*, the supervillain is General Zod. We learn that Krypton is a planet that practices eugenics, has a caste system, and has engaged in colonization of the cosmos, creating giant machines that transform other planets into environments like Krypton, obliterating whatever creatures lived there before them.

After a 100,000 year Reich, however, Krypton is in deep decline. Its colonies have failed, and the planet itself is in danger of implosion due to mining its core for energy. Two men, Jor-El and General Zod, wish to save Krypton.

Jor-El is the far-sighted scientist who warned the Kryptonians of the folly of mining their planet's core (how enlightened). Jor-El and his wife Lara have created a natural child, Kal-El, a child of choice and chance (how liberal). Jor-El then somehow hides in the genetic codes of other, as yet unborn Kryptonians in the body of Kal-El (whatever that means). Then Jor-El launches the child into space in a tiny capsule. This, somehow, will save the Kryptonian race. Sounds like a plan!

General Zod, the leader of the warrior caste, attempts to restore Krypton by launching a military coup. He wishes to extinguish the bloodlines of the rulers who have brought Krypton to its sorry state. But he is captured and exiled with his followers. But when Krypton finally implodes, they are freed. They then search the universe for Jor-El's child to recover their genetic database. They track him to Earth, which they wish to seize and "terraform" into another Krypton, so they can begin their race anew. Humanity, needless to say, will be exterminated. (Inequality + eugenics + *Lebensraum* + genocide = "Nazis.")

Superman rejects Zod's proposal in the name of egalitarian humanism. A believer in diversity and open borders, he suggests that the Kryptonians share the planet. One Kryptonian tells Superman that his morality is an evolutionary disadvantage. Kryptonians have no morality and believe only in evolution. Of course Superman's egalitarianism is not the same as "morality" as such. The Kryptonians also have a moral code, namely a kind of social Darwinism, which means that they feel no obligation to any weaker species, particularly when the very survival of their race is in peril.

Well, you can't bargain with Nazis. Remember Munich, 1938? So ray guns and bullets are discharged, blows are exchanged, spaceships and airplanes and Kryptonians whoosh around, and Metropolis is pretty much reduced to rubble, all to another thundering, tuneless, dreary Hans Zimmer score. In the end, General Zod is killed, and his followers are poofed into another dimension where they will be held in suspended animation until Alan Smithee's *Man of Steel II* comes out next summer.

The lesson of *Man of Steel* is the same lesson as practically any other superhero movie: white Americans must never dream of controlling our own destiny. Instead, we must trust in the benevolent hegemony of superheroes: a tiny, hidden minority of powerful aliens and freaks. Superheroes are the only thing that can save us from supervillains and all the evils for which they stand: inequality, eugenics, hierarchy, xenophobia, etc. In short, everything practiced by Jews to preserve their race, and everything which, if practiced by whites, would secure us against

Jewish subversion, domination, and ultimately genocide.

Counter-Currents/*North American New Right*,
June 21, 2013

SUPERMAN & THE WHITE CHRIST
AMERICAN, ALIEN, OR GOD?

GREGORY HOOD

Superman is the most American of heroes—and the most foreign. As the archetypal comic book character, Superman sets the standard for everyone else—the classic "white hat" who stands for "truth, justice, and the American Way." While complicated "dark" heroes like Batman or outright antiheroes like the Punisher can be endlessly reinterpreted or deconstructed, there's only so much one can do with the Man of Steel before changing the character entirely. To change Superman's background and beliefs (as in *Red Son*) or create a thinly veiled "evil" Superman (as in *Irredeemable*) is to simply use the unchangeable core of the character as a launching pad for meditations on the ideas of identity, heroism, and culture. Superman *is* the American hero, and if he indeed ceases to be American, it is a powerful indicator that America itself has ceased to exist as a meaningful cultural identity. While that is happening, we're not quite there.

At the same time, Superman is an alien—literally and figuratively. A creation of Jews, a foe of the Nazis who threatens the Führer with a "strictly non-Aryan sock on the jaw," Superman is both an assimilationist and supremacist fantasy. On the one hand, Superman is raised in Middle America by patriotic, plain-speaking rural folk with clean morals. The result is the flag-waving "big blue Boy Scout" who in most canon stories voluntarily serves as a tool of the American government.

On the other hand, Superman is from an alien planet, living *among*, but not *as* one of the Americans. His strength and virtue are valued only insofar as they serve the ends of the American elite, as interpreted by the moral commissars of the Lower East Side. More moral, more enlightened, more powerful, and (often quite literally) above the *goyim*, Superman as Jew is such an obvious metaphor that the National Socialists were pointing it out 70 years before comic books became the basis of college courses.[1]

In Zack Snyder's *Watchmen*, a character is quoted as having said, "The Superman exists—and he is American." Later, the character corrects that what he said was "God exists—and he is American." In *Man of Steel*, Snyder gives us a Superman/God who becomes American.

Krypton is an "Aryan" planet in appearance (no non-white Kryptonians) organized along caste lines. The planet is quite literally collapsing, as the core has been hollowed out in the quest for resources. Jor-El (Russell Crowe) is a scientist who alone has seen the catastrophe awaiting his people, and more importantly, has seen its root cause. The Kryptonians were a space-faring, expansionist people until they tried to take direct control over their reproduction. The result was a complete halt of all natural births, the end of expansion and space colonization, and cultural stagnation and death. Jor-El and his wife, as a final sign of hopeful defiance, give a natural birth to Kal-El, and send him to Earth to escape the death of their planet.

Man of Steel is predictably egalitarian in most ways. The villain is General Zod and his small team of military followers. Zod is utterly devoted to preserving the physical existence of his race. He launches a *coup* against Krypton's failed leadership and plans to extinguish their bloodlines. He respects Jor-El but kills him for stealing the key to the "codex," the genetic record of the entire

---

[1] http://www.calvin.edu/academic/cas/gpa/superman.htm

people. Finally, when he is reawakened after his *coup*, he travels to all of the space colonies, looking for any sign of survival.

In contrast, Superman (Kal-El) seems eerily indifferent to the survival of his people. When he finds out who he is, where he comes from, and what is at stake, he seems oddly troubled at the prospect of racial renewal, prompting his adoptive Earth mother to blurt out, "Isn't that [racial survival] a good thing?" After all, as his real father Jor-El notes, it is his position as an alien among the Earthlings that makes him a "god to them." To become just another Kryptonian is in some sense to strip Superman of his destiny—to make him not a Superman at all.

As a young man, we see "Clark" reading Plato's *Republic*. The *Republic* famously posits a caste system of specific classes trained to rule, with the enterprise overseen by a group of philosopher-kings. Each class is "bred" for its specific purpose and given an explanatory myth, fitting into an organic whole that is the "just" community.

Zod is the self-aware product of this kind of a system, with every action he has ever taken in his entire life justified on the grounds of the protection of his people. When Superman destroys his efforts, he destroys his very soul. Nietzsche wrote, "That which is falling should also be pushed." It could be argued that Zod is simply trying to shock life back into a dead system. If we can still use the term "human" to refer to Kryptonians, it could even be argued that Zod isn't human, but the product of a failed breeding scheme.

In contrast, Superman is given the power of choice, even defined by it. As the first natural born Kryptonian in centuries, Kal-El is not assigned a particular mission. His father outlines one for him—telling him that he will set an example for the people of earth to follow. They may stumble or fall—but he will pull them behind him.

He can be a savior for them. Jor-El rejects his own people in favor of a messianic mission for another—"You can save them all," he tells his son from beyond the grave. While Jor-El theoretically believes in choice, he dooms his son to a heavy responsibility, essentially demanding he accept his responsibility as a god.

However, "Clark" also has an Earth father, Jonathan Kent, who tells him that he doesn't owe anyone anything, even basic morality. "You're going to have to decide what kind of man you want to be," he tells his adoptive son. Jonathan Kent knows he can't physically discipline his son—he can only give the best moral teaching he can and force Clark to confront the awful responsibility of choice. When Clark uses his powers to save a school bus full of drowning children (including a boy who earlier bullied him), Jonathan Kent questions whether he did the right thing. When Clark indignantly asks if he should have let them die, Jonathan responds, "Maybe." Lest he be accused of cruelty, Jonathan later sacrifices his own life to protect his son's secret, allowing himself to be sucked into a tornado and with his last action silently commanding Clark not to reveal himself.

One key problem with the "Superman as Jew" analysis is that if Superman is an alien, he is defined by his *rejection* of his alien roots and his embrace of his folksy American upbringing. Religiously, it's canon that Superman was raised as a Methodist, and in *Man of Steel* Kal-El turns to a Christian church for comfort and guidance in his moment of crisis. It is a minister who gives the advice he will ultimately follow, a "leap of faith" to trust humanity.

General ZOG, er, Zod's plan consists of pushing out the native inhabitants of a place in order to make it safe for colonization by a new people who feel it is their right and destiny to do so. Zod even explicitly rejects offers of human/Kryptonian coexistence, which would be a sacrifice on the part of the humans, not the Kryptonians. If Superman is a "Jew," he is one who turns against his own kind, fighting to destroy the new program of interstellar Zionism.

Clearly, *Man of Steel* is not some deep anti-Zionist propaganda—Zod is an obvious stand-in for nationalism, hierarchy, militarism, and duty, all evil things that need to be destroyed by our modern democratic world. Superman stands with the weak, the victims, and the would-be dispossessed. Still, the overtly *anti-white, anti-Traditionalism* message should not disqualify Snyder's attempt to create his own unique take on the Superman character—that of the White Christ, the Aryan warrior-god who commands compassion through fear, self-sacrifice through the selfish display of power. More than that, it is a god who insists upon the power of choice, who asks that we follow him along the path to godlike behavior. But what kind of behavior does this savior ask of us?

THE WHITE CHRIST

Jesus "meek and mild" is not the God of the European peoples. Nor is it the mysterious rabbi whose esoteric teachings were rooted in various obscure schools of Jewish mysticism. As chronicled in James Russell's *The Germanization of Early Medieval Christianity*, Jesus was "sold" to the Germanic peoples as a warrior god, the dragon slayer, a more reliable guarantor of victory in battle than the treacherous Odin, who has his own agenda. After all, Loki charges the All-Father in the *Lokasenna* that he "oft has thou given to those whom thou oughtest not—victory to cowards," and Odin doesn't really deny it.

Christ as the Bringer of Victory in this world was the Savior figure of the Christianity that created the "Christendom" that launched the Crusades. It is the breakdown of this world-accepting, "pagan" Christianity that is leading to the deracinated, emasculated late American Christianity of today. In many ways, the egalitarian, anti-racist, world-denying, self-despising "faith" of liberal Christians and certain evangelicals is more faithful to the Jewish communitarian cult that was Christianity before its "Germanic" transformation.

It's fairly obvious that Zack Snyder is deliberately giving us a portrayal of Superman as Christ—he admits as much.[2] Superman is "literally Biblical," in his view. However, Snyder's Superman echoes the earlier, heroic Christianity—the all-powerful being still capable of suffering, the god intervening to save the fallen, the man slowly coming to terms with his divine nature. Henry Cavill's Superman is almost comically Aryan—all chiseled features and overwhelming amounts of muscle. This is the literal portrayal of Christ as a warrior favored by early Germanic Christians that survives in churches to this day as images of a White Christ.

Like the young Christ, Cavill's Clark Kent is aware of his awesome power (though a more physical kind of strength rather than debating Jewish law) but he restrains it. In one scene, he is being taunted but silently endures it—when he is finally left alone, he has crushed a steel bar with his hand as he struggles to hold himself back.

The mystery of Christianity (and the cause of much schism and bloodshed within the faith) is the idea God and Man are one in the person of Christ Jesus. In Nicean Christianity, He is in "being of one substance with the Father." Obviously, if Jesus was God, he could have come down from the cross—he was even challenged to do so by the Jewish priests. However, Jesus *had* to suffer and

---

[2] http://screenrant.com/zack-snyder-man-of-steel-marvel-vs-dc-superhero-movies/

die—and more importantly, freely choose this sacrifice—in order to the pay the blood atonement and absorb the wrath of God for man's sins. The nature of this sacrifice was that mankind did not "earn" it—it was freely given of God to an undeserving people. Christ could only accomplish His mission through His destruction—and resurrection.

Snyder's Superman also meets his destiny with a sacrifice. When General Zod arrives on Earth and tells the planet to produce Kal-El, only Lois Lane and his parents know who he is. Kal-El could have flown away or remained silent. Instead, he presents himself to the world, even allowing the military to go through the farce of handcuffing him "if it makes them feel more secure." He then allows himself to be delivered to Zod and makes his choice to fight him. When his ghostly father (his consciousness preserved through technology) tells him that he can save Earth, Superman flies out of a spacecraft into position above the planet, his arms stretched outward as Snyder consciously replicates the pose of crucifixion.

However, Superman's adaptation of his position as "savior" doesn't come through passive sacrifice, but through combat. He brutally battles the Kryptonians in the streets of Metropolis, utterly annihilating the city in the process. When he disables Zod's device to destroy the Earth, it requires him to use all of his power. More importantly, as Superman is fighting Kryptonians, he is essentially fighting his equals. There is no supernatural power that his sacrifice "unleashes"—he must achieve victory in this world, though physical force, and he can be defeated and killed despite his best efforts.

In the same way, those who fulfill Jor-El's hope of "following" Superman do so not through dedication, but through physical acts of courage and self-sacrifice. A military officer originally skeptical of Superman later sacrifices himself to save the city, his dying words an echo of a Kryptonian's earlier taunt—"A good death is its own reward." Perry White "follows" Superman in his own way by working to rescue one of his reporters even though such an effort will most likely lead to his own death. The path to the divine this new Superman has for us (as laid out by Jor-El) is to sacrifice everything for the people around us, and so redeem ourselves.

The problem, of course, is that Superman can do extraordinary things precisely because he is Superman. The rest of us can't fly, don't have heat vision, and can't shrug off bullets. The efforts of White and of the American military in the film would have been pointless and futile were it not for Superman's godlike powers. Self-sacrifice is a noble creed—when the only things that can kill you are your fellow gods. Now that the Kryptonians have been defeated, what can possibly stand against Superman (besides, of course, other baddies from outer space)?

Furthermore, while Superman represents a creed of everyone sacrificing for everyone else, he's not willing to live by the same rules as the rest of us. Understandably concerned about the godlike being flying around wherever he wants, the government uses a satellite to track his movements. Superman takes down the satellite, destroying millions of dollars worth of government property. He informs a military officer that he will help America but only on "my terms," and that after all, he can be trusted because he was raised in Kansas. It's a good thing no one ever raised in Kansas grew up to despise the country and inflict horrible consequences on everyone else.[3]

Ultimately, how will Superman serve an example to the rest of the people? Through service to be sure, but service mixed with intimidation and feats designed to

---

[3] http://en.wikipedia.org/wiki/Ann_Dunham

inspire awe. Superman's moral code is to be followed because he is Superman and at a level of power and strength so far above us that he can compel it. What makes him a hero is that he also chooses to impose this responsibility on himself, despite his impulses. After all, if he did otherwise, he would simply destroy cities occasionally out of resentment of the ungrateful creatures he saves (as the Plutonian in fact does to Singapore during *Irredeemable*). But the threat is always there.

Just like the Christian God, Superman gives us the promise of salvation but backed by the threat of force if we do not follow his suicidal code. It's pretty clear what Superman would do if the American government did something that violated his sense of right and wrong—after all, the Superman never kills rule went out the window when he snapped General Zod's neck.

Snyder's Superman is a warrior-god, someone to intimidate us into following "the better angels of our nature." More than that, just as in Christianity, Superman imposes (and shares) with us the terrible responsibility of choice, and the consequences that follow from making the wrong one. The idea of fate, of unchosen loyalties, or inherent natures are rejected—even Jor-El says he cannot go with his son because he is as much a part of the failed system as General Zod or Krypton's incompetent leaders. The only exception of course is Superman himself—the god who has an entire race encoded in his DNA, who has power because of who he is rather than anything he did, and the only actor whose choice actually means anything, because he can compel everyone else.

Our people followed the White Christ because they understood the idea of fealty to a greater power, loyalty to the ultimate Lord who could promise victory in this world as in the next. Unfortunately, submerged beneath the warlike aesthetics and organizational power of the Church was the poisonous egalitarian universalist creed, which ultimately eroded the faith from within in a drama that is playing out all around us. This terrible contradiction set our people against themselves, and since the French Revolution (and arguably before) we've been tearing ourselves apart.

Snyder's Superman is a White Christ who shares our struggles, understands our hatreds, and gives us victory in this world. However, ultimately, by serving as a superhuman enforcer of an egalitarian creed, he is not pulling humanity along, but holding it down.

Heidegger wrote that "Only a god can save us now." He may be right. But it won't be this god—or the creed he asks us to follow.

Counter-Currents/*North American New Right*,
June 26, 2013

BATMAN V SUPERMAN:
DAWN OF JUSTICE

TREVOR LYNCH

In any matchup between Batman and Superman, I side with Batman. I've never liked the character of Superman, because he is not a man at all. He's basically a god. He's not a human being who has raised himself to the pinnacles of human excellence. He's an alien who is simply endowed with superior abilities. There is nothing heroic about Superman, because he is almost invulnerable. He faces no risks. There's nothing he must struggle to overcome.

Batman, however, is a true Nietzschean superman, a man who has made himself more than a man. He's a man who faces injury, death, and imprisonment night after night in order to fight evil. I don't want to live in a godless universe, but frankly I would prefer that we make ourselves into gods rather than find them readymade.

I didn't like Zack Synder's first Superman movie, *Man of Steel*, so I had very low expectations for *Batman v Superman: Dawn of Justice*. That said, for the first 80% of *Batman v Superman*, I found myself thinking this is a pretty good movie. Zack Snyder would be a great silent movie director, and the opening credit sequence (based on Frank Miller's *The Dark Knight Returns* graphic novel) is pure poetry. The first appearance of the Batman is genuinely terrifying. There is a great nightmare sequence in which Batman fights against Superman's henchmen who are dressed as Nazi soldiers while giant cockroach-Valkyries whisk the fallen to some sort of hellish Valhalla. The directing, editing, and special effects throughout are superb. Hans Zimmer's score, moreover, is one of his better efforts. But for all that, at about the 2-hour mark, the movie became ludicrous, unintelligible, and uninvolving.

The movie is set about two years after *Man of Steel*. The public is souring on Superman. Sure, he saved the earth from the Kryptonians, but a lot was destroyed in the process. And maybe the Kryptonians came here because of him. And he is one of them too. How can we trust him? How do we know he will always be benevolently disposed to us? Is Superman outside the law? Shouldn't he have to follow the same laws as the rest of us? Superman may look human, but he is not. Shouldn't we fear a god who has no real attachment humanity?

Three of Superman's critics are Senator June Finch (Holly Hunter), billionaire Lex Luthor (Jesse Eisenberg, whose characterization is a cross between Zorg from *The Fifth Element* and the Joker from *The Dark Knight*), and billionaire Bruce Wayne (Ben Affleck), who moonlights as Batman. For his part, Superman's alter-ego, Clark Kent, sees Batman as a dangerous vigilante. There are also conflicts between Luthor and Senator Finch, who refuses to allow him to import kryptonite, and between Luthor and Batman, who steals the kryptonite after it is smuggled in.

Conflict, of course, is the stuff of good plots. But characterization is essential too. Unfortunately, Luthor's motives are the murkiest, which is unfortunate, because he drives the entire plot. Luthor gets Lois Lane taken hostage by African revolutionaries, knowing Superman will come to her rescue. Then he has mercenaries massacre the guerrillas, and Superman is blamed. Luthor tries to acquire kryptonite to use against Superman, but it is blocked by Finch then stolen by Batman. Luthor bombs a Senate hearing at which Superman is testifying. Superman, of course, survives but is humiliated and disappears for a while.

When Superman returns, Luthor gets Batman and Superman to fight one another. Batman, however, is prepared for the fight with new armor and kryptonite weapons, which significantly weaken Superman. However, when Batman is poised to kill Superman with a kryptonite spear, he pauses at the last minute when Superman says "Martha," his mother's name—which, coincidentally, is the name of Bruce Wayne's mother as well. Then Lois Lane arrives to explain that Superman has been blackmailed into fighting Batman by Luthor, who has kidnapped Martha Kent. Then the two superheroes unite to fight Luthor and rescue Martha.

Now, this sort of peripety is the stuff of classic drama and grand opera and Bollywood. Yes, it is ludicrous when stated baldly, but it doesn't have to seem that way. It could have been handled well. It almost works as it is. But it also marks the point when the movie stopped working.

After Superman and Batman team up to fight Luthor, he unleashes his final assault. Using technology from a crashed Kryptonian vessel, Luthor has created a monster (basically an electrified version of Peter Jackson's cave trolls) that is capable of destroying Superman.

Batman and Superman are then joined in their epic battle by Wonder Woman, played by Israeli actress Gal Gadot. Although I admit that my reaction is not entirely rational, given the amount of disbelief I had already suspended, I found the addition of another superhero intensely annoying. I had the same reaction to *Twilight*. I was fine with the vampires but thought the whole thing was ruined by adding werewolves.

Superman realizes that the troll, like him, is vulnerable only to kryptonite, so he uses Batman's kryptonite spear to kill it. Unfortunately, using the spear also weakens Superman, whom the beast kills in its death throes.

To my great surprise, when Batman began to deploy

his kryptonite weapons against Superman, weakening him to the point that he could have been killed, I found myself *liking* Superman more. It makes sense, though, because to be vulnerable is to be human. But to fight on in spite of vulnerability is true heroism. Before this, Superman may have been super, but he was no hero, because he was invulnerable. Invulnerable men, however, do not face risks, require virtues, or make sacrifices. And when at the movie's climax Superman *risks death* and then *actually dies* to save us, it had a real emotional punch. And when all the whooshing and zapping dies down and the movie shifts into *dénouement* mode, it somewhat recovers.

Lex Luthor is imprisoned (and when his head is shaved looks like a rat), Superman is memorialized, Clark Kent is buried back in Kansas, and Batman joins Wonder Woman to search for other "metahumans" like herself, since after Superman's death the earth is vulnerable to other threats that lie beyond. I smell franchise.

But it appears that they will have some help after all, for in the last shot of the film, a few particles of earth thrown on the lid of Clark Kent's coffin begin to levitate. Yes, that's right, Superman did not just die to save mankind, he will rise from the dead to continue the fight. This confirms Gregory Hood's reading of *Man of Steel* as offering Superman as an Aryan warrior Christ.

Superman's experience of vulnerability to kryptonite was, in effect, his incarnation—his descent from being an immortal god to being a mortal man—in order that he could die for our salvation. And his impending resurrection is a return to divine status, although this time he will also have a connection to humanity, because he lived and died as one of us, which makes him far less threatening.

Zack Snyder is an extraordinarily talented director. *Watchmen* remains the greatest superhero movie ever made. But it had an excellent script, a script that even improved upon the original graphic novel. The best director in the world can't overcome a bad script though, and Snyder's recent works, from *Sucker Punch* to the Superman movies, suffer from bad scripts.

In terms of performances, Jesse Eisenberg's Luthor was more a collection of quirks than a character. Henry Cavill and Ben Affleck look better than they act. Gal Gadot's Wonder Woman isn't even good-looking.

The Christian allegory in Snyder's Superman films is an interesting dimension. *Batman v Superman* is relatively free of political correctness. But it is also free of the philosophical depth and Rightist political themes of Nolan's Dark Knight Trilogy. Although the portrayal of Luthor as a shrimpy, neurotic, fast-talking Jewboy who manipulates two hulking white superheroes into trying to kill each other does have an archetypal quality that gives one pause.

After a strong opening week, *Batman v Superman* sank like kryptonite. Let's hope it is the end of the franchise and Zack Snyder finds a better outlet for his considerable talent. He's actually talking about remaking *The Fountainhead*, for instance. (Snyder and Christopher Nolan would be among my top picks for a proper *Atlas Shrugged* adaptation as well.) Until then, he remains on artistic probation.

Counter-Currents/*North American New Right*,
May 25, 2016

JUSTICE LEAGUE

TREVOR LYNCH

Watchmen is the greatest superhero movie of all time,[1] and when it was released, its director Zack Snyder was poised to follow Christopher Nolan into the first rank of directors working today. But instead, he has directed an ever worsening series of turkeys: *Sucker Punch, Man of Steel, Batman v Superman,* and now *Justice League,* which is one of the worst movies I have ever seen: derivative, dumb, and dull. An assault on the senses and an insult to the intellect. It is also one of the most expensive movies ever made, costing an astonishing $300 million. It is really rather amazing that a director of Snyder's proven talent, with a solid cast and a $300 million budget, could not have turned in a better movie. Clearly, there's a lot of rot and a lot of ruin still left in Hollywood, and the sex scandals are just the beginning.

Justice League is a critical and commercial flop. Some people are trying to deflect the blame onto Warner Bros. and Joss Whedon. It turns out that earlier this year, Snyder's 20-year-old Chinese adopted daughter, Autumn, committed suicide. (Snyder had eight children, four natural and four adopted.) Snyder took some time off to be with his family, and Warner Bros., which deemed the movie too long and too dark, brought in Joss Whedon for rewrites and reshoots. The problem, howev-

---

[1] See Trevor Lynch, "Watchmen," https://www.countercurrents.com/2017/05/watchmen/. See also my reviews of 300 in *Trevor Lynch's White Nationalist Guide to the Movies* and *Sucker Punch* in *Son of Trevor Lynch's White Nationalist Guide to the Movies*.

er, is not with Whedon's superficial changes but with the basic script, which is utterly derivative, and with the characterization, which is laughably shallow.

Stop me if you've heard this one before. In remotest antiquity, a dark lord from another world named Steppenwolf (hold your laughter) tried to conquer the world with the aid of three magical "Mother Boxes" and an army of zombie-cyborgs called parademons. However, the races of the earth—the Olympian gods, Amazons, Atlanteans, and men—came together in an alliance to defeat him. The Mother Boxes were wrested away from Steppenwolf, who vanished. The Mother Boxes, which only worked in tandem, were then separated and placed in the care of the Atlanteans, the Amazons, and the kings of men.

After untold thousands of years, however, the death of Superman somehow reactivated the mother boxes, which called Steppenwolf back to earth. Of course, this is a ridiculously arbitrary plot turn, since Superman was only a recent arrival on earth, which raises the question of what kept the Mother Boxes "sleeping" for the untold millennia before his arrival. But never mind. The dark lord Steppenwolf is back with his parademons searching for the magic Mother Boxes that will allow him to conquer the world. To stop him, a league must be created, bringing together an Atlantean (Aquaman), an Amazon (Wonder Woman), and several humans, including Bruce Wayne/Batman, Barry Allen/Flash, and Victor Stone/Cyborg.

Yes, thus far, it is just a retelling of *The Fellowship of the Ring*.

But the combined efforts of the Justice League are still not enough to defeat Steppenwolf, so a *deus ex machina* is required. Thus they use one of the Mother Boxes to resurrect Superman, who whooshes in to save the day. There are lots of CGI battles, which basically feel like being trapped inside a pinball machine, and finally Steppenwolf is sent packing, no doubt to return some day when bidden by the dark lords of Hollywood to harvest more shekels from the *goyim*.

Okay, Okay. But aren't there are only so many plots? And can't a derivative plot still be salvaged by interesting characters and dialogue? This is true, but *Justice League* fails there as well. We have already been introduced to Batman, Superman, and Wonder Woman. Thus all Snyder really needed to do was breathe some life into Aquaman, Cyborg, and Flash. And what a lousy job he does. Aquaman is the most one-dimensional character of all. He is covered with tattoos, has long hair, and swigs whiskey from a bottle. So we know he's badass. He's angry at his mommy. He likes to help people for some reason, but thinks he does it best alone. Cyborg is a black man with a stratospherically high IQ which he inherited from his black scientist father. No regression to the mean in this universe. And Flash, just like Lex Luthor in the last movie, is a shrimpy, neurotic, fast-talking, cowardly Jewboy. (What's Zack Snyder trying to tell us?) There's no depth, nuance, subtlety, or humanity in *Justice League*, just plastic robots, batteries not included. The established characters also seem hollowed out and flattened. But with no human beings at its core, the movie's CGI battle scenes become a tedious, emotionally uninvolving assault on the senses.

One of the running theses of my career as a movie reviewer is that someone in Hollywood is reading antimodern, Traditionalist Rightists and recognizes that we represent the most fundamental negation of liberal humanism and thus the perfect supervillains. *Justice League* nods in this direction at the beginning when Wonder Woman foils a group of white "reactionary" terrorists who want to blow up the Old Bailey in London. Also, under the opening credits, which are a montage of social chaos after the death of Superman to a cover of Leonard Cohen's "Everybody Knows," we see a white man with shaved head menacing a shopkeeper in a hijab and her child. But like everything else in this film, even this feels perfunctory, phoned-in, and fake.

I hope the failure of this movie and the suicide of his daughter will cause Zack Snyder to take some time away from Hollywood to rethink his career. The great weaknesses of his recent films have been plot and characterization. His best films, 300 and *Watchmen*, were based on classic graphic novels, and from that high starting point, he actually improved upon them, both in terms of visualization and plot. But Snyder's career since then seems almost like a controlled experiment to establish that all the directorial and technical wizardry in the world can't make a compelling movie if the plot and characterization are lacking, nor can brand-loyalty and PR-puffery turn it into a success.

The fact that *Justice League* has bombed is proof that there is still some justice in the world.

Counter-Currents/*North American New Right*,
November 28, 2017

THE ALT KNIGHT:
A RETROSPECT OF FRANK MILLER'S *THE DARK KNIGHT RETURNS* FOR THE CURRENT YEAR[*]

ZACHARY O. RAY

Sometime in the near future, in an America crippled by degeneracy and stifling bureaucracy, two men of stature fight in the streets. One, an aging billionaire fed up with his society's imminent collapse, has become a polarizing threat to the governing establishment. The other, a compromised but well-meaning foreigner wrapped in an American flag, bringing a false and used-up patriotism to a disenfranchised population.

The men I speak of are not Donald Trump and Ted Cruz, but the World's Finest themselves—Batman and Superman.

In this future, your average American might look into the sky as an object flies overhead, but it'd just be a bird or a plane. The era of the superhero is over—their presence banned as a threat to democratic normalcy. The Cold War is hotter than history has recorded. Meanwhile, Gotham is slowly succumbing to the decay of street gangs and low-energy politicians too incompetent or comfortable to bother themselves. Homeless doomsayers trudge through the streets prophesying the end times. The superhero has been reduced to the realm of legend for young generations, who, with no heroes of their own, are drawn to the seductive promises of miscreant gang chieftains.

Published in 1986, Frank Miller's *The Dark Knight Re-*

---

[*] http://plugging-out.blogspot.com/2016/09/the-alt-knight-retrospect-of-frank.html

turns breathed life into a comic-book industry suffocated by the creativity-killing censorship of the self-imposed Comics Code Authority (not so different from the "private" censorship of social media today). DKR not only ushered in an era of creative vitality, bringing a dying medium back to its feet, but to this day it serves as a clever and relevant work of modern satire. The Cold War may be over, but just as in Miller's dystopia, we're living in a Kali Yuga—an age void of heroes, when eccentric mediocrities are fetishized by the 20-square-inch boxes in our living rooms, and all hope is almost lost . . . almost.

While every work of art is defined by the vision of its artist, there comes a point in the life cycle of all great works where art takes on a new life beyond its author's intent—a point in which the piece no longer belongs to the author, but to the culture.

In this sense, *The Dark Knight Returns* serves as an Alt Right hero's journey, in so far as it chronicles Western man's spiritual struggle towards superhuman reawakening against modern egalitarian mediocrity—including a necessary break from American conservatism. It is a battle cry, not just for a creative revolution in the stuffy recesses of the comic book medium, but a call to arms against the existential lethargy of modern man.

THE BAT PILL

> "The time has come. You know it in your soul. For I am your soul . . . You cannot escape me . . . you are puny, you are small—you are nothing—a hollow shell, a rusty trap that cannot hold me . . . you cannot stop me—not with wine or vows or the weight of age—you cannot stop me but but still you try—still you run—you try to drown me out—but your voice is weak . . ."

Enter billionaire Bruce Wayne, age 55. Ten years ago, he hung up his cape and cowl—swearing an oath he would never don them again. A restrained titan among Last Men, his purposeless life draws on, as he drinks by himself during the day, dreaming of a perfect death—a perfect death to take away the pain—the pain of watching his beloved Gotham City slowly sink into the abyss of rot and chaos—as good men do nothing.

All that is left for the former crime fighter is nostalgia and baseless thrill-seeking. Behind what appears to be a life of futility broods a malevolent demon—the Batman persona incarnate, transcending masked vigilantism and biological decrepitude—urging, no, compelling the fruitless Bruce Wayne to become who he is. No longer can Bruce Wayne stand by as news station after news station regurgitates the same deterministic and sanitized murder stories. As we are learning today, Wayne can ignore reality no longer.

The threat is here and it is time to act. In a blaze of glory, Batman sweeps the streets of Gotham—revitalizing hope in Gotham's citizenry.

There is little doubt that Miller, the man who called Occupy Wall Street "nothing but a pack of louts, thieves, and rapists" and author of the unabashedly identitarian 300 and "Islamophobic" *Holy Terror*, was channeling many of the same concerns back in 1986 that the Alternative Right is facing today. While the West is certainly sick, it is a sickness it has brought on itself. Unlike European colonialism in the 19th century, the Global South's colonialism today is strictly the result of the self-imposed ethnomasochism of a civilization defeated by centuries of victory (to paraphrase Bane from *The Dark Knight Rises*) and internal warring.

While DKR is not, by any means, a commentary on modern immigration, it challenges the same wounded spirit of the modern world. Like his fellow supermen in tights, Batman quit because he chose to quit. There was no one to stop him. He gave up by his own volition, but something deep inside him urges that the war goes on.

A REFLECTION

> "I close my eyes and listen. Not fooled by sight, I see him . . . as he is. I see him. I see . . . a reflection."

Due to Batman's successful return to crime fighting and subsequent public approval, a coalition consisting of the media, politicians, and "public intellectuals" arises devoted to stamping out the new public champion threatening their authority. Sound familiar?

Arkham Asylum Home for the Emotionally Troubled releases two of Batman's greatest foes, Two-Face and the Joker, upon psychological evaluation by Dr. Bartholmew Wolper—a curly black-haired, whiny, and narcissistic psychoanalyst, who occupies the airwaves crying out against the "reactionary" crime fighting of the Dark Knight, while he sits cozily in a television recording studio in his pali sandals, ironic (or not so ironic) toothbrush mustache, and Superman t-shirt.

Wolper, accompanied by the narrative of the mainstream media, inspires the release of the two by demanding that they are not murderous villains, but misunderstood outsiders victimized by Batman's "fascist obsessions." As is customary, soon after their releases, both go on the greatest terroristic murder sprees of their careers. (It's worth noting that Dent's plan involves blowing up Gotham's "Twin Towers"—mind you, this was written in 1986.)

Even Wolper, the primary advocate behind the anti-Batman controversy and release of Gotham's most dangerous, is murdered by the Joker on a live late-night talk show, as a public relations attempt to clear the Joker's name goes awry.

Like the refugees in Europe and the Black Lives Matter crowd, the Joker knows how to game the progressive establishment. He has been crystal clear in his unwillingness to live peacefully in society, yet the metropolitan liberals refuse to see this. A great irony of Islam's disdain toward the West is that it is derived from the very "weak horses" (to borrow from the Lion Sheik himself) who defend Muslims at every turn.

Like Leftists today, Wolper defends civilization's enemies, despite the fact that it is the likes of him who they hate most of all.

To move on to the central point, the irony of Batman and the Joker lies in their stark contradictions. One, a hero, looks like a brooding monster; the other, who looks like a childhood circus performer, is a mass-murdering maniac. As Nolan's *The Dark Knight* captures perfectly, the Joker is chaos incarnate. He is the Dionysus to Batman's Apollo. Batman's recurring conflict with the Joker represents his attempt to bring order to the randomness of existence that took the lives of his parents. Batman is the virility that is birthed in the midst of chaos. Just as the Joker only awoke from a coma upon hearing of Batman's return—a coma that was induced by Batman's disappearance from the public eye—Batman cannot exist in a world without chaos (embodied in the Joker).

Western man is no different. Western man reaches his potential only when his back is against the wall. The refugee crisis, and the innumerable attacks and rapes that have followed, though an immediate threat to our long-term existence, could be just the thing to spawn a new flowering era in Western history.

It's worth recognizing that Miller initially frames Batman's moral crusade, quite true to character, as one of *ressentiment*. The very Batman persona, itself, grew out of Bruce Wayne's deep-seated frustration with the seemingly unintelligible disarray of life's suffering. It is for this very reason that Batman's existence has been thematically bound to the Joker over the decades. Batman exists so that he can create a world where he will not have to exist. For many identitarians, it's easy to fall into this same temptation—hating one's enemy more than loving one's own.

But by the climax of the penultimate issue, Batman paralyzes the Joker, who subsequently commits suicide to frame him. Batman has now overcome his greatest existential threshold. His journey must now be self-fulfilling, self-perpetuating, or he must die. The manhunt for the Batman that ensues only confirms the inevitable—that Batman's crusade must take on the establishment sooner or later.

Two-Face also reflects Batman's persona. After finally being apprehended, Dent tragically reveals that despite his recent plastic surgery to correct his disfigured face—a procedure funded by Wayne himself in a naïve humanitarian attempt to rehabilitate his old foe—Dent's shadow-self has overcome him entirely. This symbolic gesture foreshadows Wayne's own transformation: in a conflict of wills (Wayne vs. Batman), it is inevitable for one to win out in the end. This is true not just within the soul, but in the world.

Conservatism fails for this reason. Deep inside, every conservative recognizes nature's iron law of inequality, masked by the current year's egalitarian paradigm. Conservatism making the way for the much purer and harder Alt Right was only a matter of time.

THE WAY OF THE GANG IS THE WAY OF THE DEMON

> "They can't be arrested. You could never hold them all. They have to be defeated. Humiliated."

In between his conflict with his old foes, Batman confronts the Mutant Gang (who are not actual mutants by the way). He recognizes that to beat them he must crush their head. After Batman beats the Mutant leader to a bloody pulp, the disillusioned Mutant Gang, with their proverbial god now proverbially dead, soon dissolves (reminiscent of the decapitation of Thulsa Doom in *Conan the Barbarian*). Unlike in *Conan*, however—and in a way much more accurate to human nature—many of the former gang members find in their enemy a new god worthy of their reverence. Donning woad and jackboots, the Sons of Batman cult is born—devoted to mercilessly crushing crime and those too cowardly to fight it themselves. More on them later . . .

SUPERHUMAN, ALL TOO SUPERHUMAN

> "'Yes'—you always say yes—to anyone with a badge—or a flag."

As his name suggests, Superman was in fact named after the *Übermensch* from Friedrich Nietzsche's *Thus Spoke Zarathustra*. Writing in a time when Nietzsche was more closely associated with the fascistic tenets of National Socialism, Jewish cartoonists Jerry Siegel and Joe Shuster sought to reshape the "Superman" in their image. No longer the hierarchical freethinker of insurmountable willpower, their Superman™ was an egalitarian strongman, an alien, whose might lay not in his will but raw materialistic faculties. Like the neoconservative establishment, Superman is a foreign entity wrapped in our flag.

Originally depicted as a hard-boiled "champion of the oppressed" in 1938, at the dawn of America's entrance into the Second World War, Superman, with Old Glory and bald eagle in hand, became a distinctly American icon alongside Uncle Sam and Lady Liberty. The Man of Steel became a symbol of "American exceptionalism"—his red and blue uniform inspired young boys to scrounge up scraps of metal in the streets for democracy's war effort.

Copies of the monthly *Superman* comic book featured the Big Blue Cheese whopping Hitler to a pulp with his fists. When Superman punched Hitler in the jaw, it was as if we were punching Hitler in the jaw. And that was good enough for us.

What happens when you run out of bad guys? Such a dilemma is explored in DKR. Superman is still the same walking propaganda poster he has always been. Here Miller treats him subversively. In DKR, America is, much as it is today, a flabby managerial state, flimsily held together by the flag and the people's bourgeois unwillingness to resist force, micromanaging the *status quo* and stamping out anything opposing it. Unlike the rest of his fellow superhumans, Superman is still at large—but only because he is on the US government's payroll.

For decades, virginal nerds have been arguing over who would win in a showdown between Batman and Superman. Recently it has been fascinating to watch fewer and fewer relate to Superman and more to Batman. This says something about our culture. Like the conservative establishment of today, fighting for "truth, justice, and the American way" isn't enough anymore.

Modern culture, or anti-culture, as it should more appropriately be called, shuns truth. "Justice," as it is defined today, has been reduced to "virtue signaling" and guilt tripping. And what exactly is "the American way" anymore?

SUPERMAN™ VERSUS SUPERMAN

> "You sold us out, Clark. You gave them the power—that should have been ours. Just like your parents taught you to. My parents taught me a different lesson—lying on this street—shaking in deep shock—

dying for no reason at all—they showed me that the world only makes sense when you force it to."

In *Angus*, George C. Scott says "Superman isn't brave. Superman is indestructible, and you can't be brave if you're indestructible." Perhaps Superman is, in fact, a perfect description of modern America. For the past century, Americans have had the privilege of being the big kid on the block. Geographically we have the protection of the world's two largest oceans. However, for the first time since perhaps the War of 1812, America is beginning to taste nonexistence. Victory, and the spoils of war, have defeated America. For so long Superman had the comfort of knowing no one posed an immediate threat to his existence.

Once this changes, he doesn't know what to do. How was it possible for mighty Rome to fall into oblivion while the tiny Jews, persecuted and bounced around through history, are as old as history itself? Why is Europe, at its height of scientific discovery, succumbing to the barbarism of a bunch of brown goblins who haven't moved past the Middle Ages?

When you don't know suffering you won't be ready for it when it arrives.

Miller's reinvented Batman, however, is a superman in the Nietzschean sense—beginning as a disaffected Gothamite, by the end he transforms into more than just a man. Unconcerned over the well-being of the *status quo* and democracy, as societal order breaks down due to nuclear detonation by the Soviets, it is Batman, with the "Sons of Batman" (former disaffected youths to whom he has given purpose) at his command, who takes the reigns of authority and declares "Tonight, I am the law!" as Gotham is consumed in fire and chaos.

Earlier, despite his highly weaponized, and expensive, equipment, Wayne couldn't even defeat a brute gang lord.

Now, a spiritually awakened Batman is taking on the most physically powerful threat on Earth, and wins in the showdown that made the "Superman vs. Batman" debate exist in the first place. When Superman fan boys bellyache that "the only reason Batman could beat Superman is because Batman is willing to do what Superman isn't," they are conceding that Batman is more powerful. Power is the ability to change, to force, to will. It doesn't matter how much intelligence or capital you have, if you aren't willing to use it what good are you?

Batman, having proven the establishment's illegitimacy by cleaning up their country better than they ever could, forces the ventriloquists to bring out their mightiest puppet, the Man of Steel, in a last-ditch effort to stomp him out once and for all.

Gone are the days of punching Hitler in the jaw.

In that climactic street fight, Superman rips Batman's helmet off, stripping away his masked identity and exposing his human identity to the world. No longer does Batman need a mask. Bruce Wayne is of no more value—there is no longer anything to hide. This consummates his becoming.

THE DARK KNIGHT AS THE THIRD WAY

"I couldn't judge it. It was too big. He was too big..."

What we're witnessing today in the United States is an establishment whose elites, caught up in a political paradigm limited by a bipartite party system, are finding themselves with their pants down when faced with alternative, non-centrist, third-way politics. You can choose rootless multiculturalism on the Left or rootless globalism on the Right but nothing else. Until recently, this has been the paradigm of the age.

The Dark Knight Returns is sprinkled with panels of

television broadcasters arguing over the exploits of the recently resurfaced Caped Crusader. For some, talking heads and citizenry alike, he is a menace to the established order—an "outdated fascist reactionary." To others he is a patriotic Minute Man of sorts, restoring Gotham to its *status quo*. But like the Alt Right of today, he is so much more than this. He is a revolt against the modern world altogether and all its bourgeois insecurities. And as he learns by the end of the novel, he must "bring sense to a world plagued by worse than thieves and murderers." Batman is in a spiritual war—first within himself, now the world, and in order to change the world, just as his spirit was reborn in the cave, his flesh must be "reborn" to take on the world. Batman was good while it lasted, but like all life, it must either die or evolve.

By the end, Batman realizes that there is more wrong with the world than street crime. The problem with it is the world itself, and in order to reestablish a sense to its madness, the only solution is to let go of this life and, as Jack Donovan might say, start the world. Batman won the streets by defeating its leader. He must win the world by defeating its leaders as well.

When it comes down to it, that's what makes the Alt Right so vital. Conserving the *status quo* is no longer sufficient—for the *status quo* does not belong to us anymore. It belongs to the Last Men and spiritual rejects. If we are to win, we must refuse to accept death, no matter how glorious it may be, as our end game. We must instead reaffirm life and order, toward a rebirth.

By the end, no longer is Bruce Wayne awaiting a good death. No. There is no future in death. He, as a superman, is in search of a good life—a life void of mediocre leaders, a life where heroes will once again roam the skies.

BATMAN:
THE DARK KNIGHT RETURNS

TREVOR LYNCH

Batman: The Dark Knight Returns is an animated movie adaptation of Frank Miller's graphic novel *The Dark Knight Returns*. Released in two 76-minute parts in 2012 and 2013, then combined into a 148-minute edition DVD and Blu-ray, this is lame, sclerotic, constipated, Z-grade animation drawn out to paralyzing lengths, completely lacking the visual style and dynamism of the original graphic novel, which is more animated on the printed page than in this adaptation.

Why review it, then? The original graphic novel seems quite paradoxical. The characters of Batman and Commissioner Gordon are highly Right-wing, truly off-the-charts on the F-scale. But this is counter-balanced by a number of features that can only be described as politically correct: anti-racist, anti-sexist, and anti-homophobic. What ties these two dimensions together is Miller's Right-wing individualism. His Rightist values are universal principles that can be followed by anyone, regardless of race, sex, etc., and it is only permissible to go outside the law in service of these values. The film, although it mostly detracts from the graphic novel, also adds a few touches that heighten its Right-wing dimensions.

After the death of Jason Todd (the second Robin), Bruce Wayne retired from the role of Batman at the age of 45. Ten years later, Gotham is at the mercy of the Mutant gang (which is, ludicrously, all-white and practically all-blond, as are practically all the other criminals in Gotham). Commissioner Gordon is 70 and on the brink of retirement. The Joker is catatonic in Arkham Asylum.

Harvey Dent/Two-Face receives reconstructive surgery courtesy of Bruce Wayne. Dent is declared sane, released from Arkham, and promptly drops out of sight and returns to crime.

Bored with retirement and appalled by the crime wave, the 55-year-old Bruce Wayne dons cape and cowl and returns to fighting crime. On one of his patrols, Batman rescues teenage girl Carrie Kelley from the Mutants. Kelley then buys a Robin costume and goes into crime fighting, eventually winning the trust of Batman. Kelley's character is an obvious concession to feminism, and, with her short hair and tomboyish demeanor, to lesbianism as well.

Batman eventually defeats Two-Face and the leader of the Mutants. Some former Mutant gang members rename themselves the Sons of Batman and become vigilantes. This disturbs President Ronald Reagan—portrayed as a sinister, greenish Frankenstein monster—who asks Superman to step in and stop Batman. Superman threatens Bruce Wayne, telling him to go back into retirement, then zooms off to Corto Maltese to fight the Soviets. Commissioner Gordon retires, and his replacement Ellen Yindel (feminist, lesbian, and very probably Jewish) issues a warrant for Batman's arrest.

Meanwhile, Batman's return has awakened the Joker from his catatonic state. Psychiatrist Bartholomew Wolper, who previously certified Harvey Dent sane and has publicly argued that Batman is actually guiltier than the criminals he fights, now champions the Joker, declaring that he had been cured and should be reintegrated into society. Wolper reintroduces the Joker to the world on a late-night talk show, but it does not go as planned. The Joker slashes Wolper's throat on live TV, then gasses the entire audience to death and escapes.

Batman tracks the Joker to an amusement park and beats him within an inch of his life. Batman knows that he could have prevented every murder committed by the

Joker since his release if he only had the strength to kill him years before. But even now, Batman cannot bring himself to simply execute the Joker. Instead, he plans to turn him over to the system that had just let him out to kill again. But the Joker does the right thing for the wrong reason. Out of sheer spite, he snaps his own neck, knowing that Batman will be accused of his murder. Batman, however, makes a narrow escape.

The Corto Maltese war escalates into a Soviet nuclear strike. Superman deflects a nuclear missile to a deserted place, but the detonation causes an electro-magnetic pulse that shuts down all electronic equipment, plunging America into chaos. Batman rallies the Sons of Batman to restore order to Gotham, making it the safest place in the nation. Reagan is embarrassed by this and orders Superman to stop Batman.

Batman and Superman then square off. Batman is strengthened by a mechanical exo-suit, and Superman is weakened by the nuclear blast and a kryptonite-tipped arrow, leading to Batman's victory. (All this is reworked in Zack Snyder's *Batman v Superman*.) Batman then dies of a heart attack, Alfred Pennyworth dies of a stroke, Wayne Manor is destroyed, and Batman is revealed to be Bruce Wayne. In the epilogue, however, we discover that Batman/Wayne faked his death and plans to carry on his crusade against crime in secret.

The portrayals of Wolper and the Joker are the most politically incorrect aspects of the movie, pushing it almost into Alt-Right territory. Wolper is a Jewish name, and he is drawn with a big nose and a black Jew-fro. In the movie, this impression is driven home by voicing him as a smarmy, liberal New York Jew. As for the Joker, he is voiced as a snarky, sibilant, effeminate homosexual.

The most substantive Right-wing elements in the film were already present in the graphic novel, of course, but seeing them on the screen had much more impact.

First, when Jason Todd's death is mentioned, the expectation is that Batman/Bruce Wayne will affirm the bourgeois assumption that nothing is worse than the violent death of a young man. But Wayne rejects this assumption at root, saying that Jason was "a soldier." Wayne's unspoken assumption is that it is appropriate for soldiers to give their lives for a cause, because there are some values higher than the preservation of individual life.

Second, when the retired Commissioner Gordon meets with his successor Ellen Yindel, he makes an extraordinary case for going outside the law for reasons of state, to pursue a higher good. He recounts how the Japanese attack on Pearl Harbor shocked Americans into entering World War II and recounts how it was later revealed that Roosevelt knew the attack was coming and did nothing to stop it, precisely to get the United States into the war. Many innocent men died, but Gordon clearly believes that Roosevelt did the right thing, even though he is not willing to come out and say it. Instead, he says that he could not judge it, because "It was too big. He was too big." Yindel only sees the relevance to Batman later, when she gives up her pursuit of him because "He's too big."

Of course, Roosevelt's ploy to get the United States to bleed for Jewry in another World War became the template for the conspiracy to get the United States to go to war with Israel's enemies in the Middle East. This, coupled with Miller's politically correct views of race and sex, gives *The Dark Knight Returns* a distinctly neoconservative ideological flavor: a marriage of liberal-democratic and globalist values with Schmittian political realism. But this is consistent with the larger superhero genre, in which Nietzschean Supermen, or just plain Supermen, always work to promote egalitarian humanism.

It's time for Batman to shrug.

Counter-Currents/*North American New Right*,
May 5, 2018

BATMAN & THE JOKER

JONATHAN BOWDEN

The Brave and the Bold
A Team-up comic featuring Batman and the Joker
DC Comics, No. 111, March 1974

This comic was published in 1974 by DC comics or National Periodical Publications. It retailed for twenty cents, and I bought it in the United Kingdom for eight new pence. The author was the veteran scripter Bob Haney, and it was drawn by Jim Aparo. None of the other contributors—the inker, colorist, letterer, or editor—is recorded.

The whole point of looking at this comic is that it dovetails with Trevor Lynch's review of the film *The Dark Knight* elsewhere in this volume. Yet there are important differences—the directness or crudity of the form, its clientele of adolescent boys, and the amount of censorship it was under pulls it in a dissimilar direction.

There is no room for the Joker, his arch nemesis, to philosophize about Batman falling short as a superman. For the very insistent dualism or absence of moral relativism means that the Joker's actions—not his words—are depicted in a despicable light. But this has an unintentional result, in that it makes Batman less liberal, more ferocious, vengeful, and "fascistic." The center of gravity then shifts, and the police commissioner, Gordon, is forever trying to restrict Gotham's finest, curb him from vigilantism, and keep him on the straight and narrow.

The story involves the Joker wiping out a totally respectable family who had the temerity to inform on a criminal. He did it as a response to normal society and as a sort of Stirnerite *aporia*—a nihilistic and anti-social act. Batman is outraged and swears an implacable vengeance. He threatens to Gordon that he will kill this sadistic clown once and for all. Gordon sniffs: "We're here to represent the Law, Batman, no vigilante stuff." To which Batman sneers: "You better find him first if you want to bring him in alive!"

There then occurs several quite complicated somersaults or backflips in the plot—thereby confirming that comics are very close to both film and television, being heavily plot-driven. The Joker allegedly returns to Gotham's morgue in order to mutilate his victims with the rictus leer which is his trademark. Why? Had he forgotten to do so?

Gradually, via an underworld tip-off, Batman tracks the purple-clad and green-haired minstrel to a lonely gravel barge (now disused). Another clue leads to a Turkish steam bath where he pounces upon the Joker as he hunts an underworld killer called Slade. Batman is wounded in the encounter, but survives.

Little by little, it dawns on Commissioner Gordon and Batman that the Joker is innocent, that he's hunting the real slayer, Slade, and that to capture the latter will involve *collaborating with the Joker*. (Note: Is there, no matter how subliminally, a notion of wartime collaboration here? Who knows?)

The Joker and Batman contact each other so as to bring home the ghastly deed to Slade. The Joker taunts and berates Batman throughout—yet there remains this strange attraction, symmetry, and false "completeness" between them. After various shenanigans, involving a chase sequence following the auction of an old gangster's Cadillac, the final element of the drama supervenes.

Throughout all of this, though, Batman has become more and more maniacal. He strong-arms criminals, roughs up a morgue attendant, disobeys police orders, is placed under arrest by Gordon ("see that Batman doesn't leave this room"), and plots openly to murder the Joker.

I believe that a comic like this has to be as either/or . . . or as Manichean as possible, morally speaking. A film can be 18 or X-certificate, and the era of graphic novels "suggested for the mature reader" didn't exist then. All mainstream comics were severely vetted or controlled and subject to a censorship board—just like in early Hollywood. Hence we see the moniker which appeared on the front of such works that read "Approved by the Comics Code Authority."

Such strictures often led to barely suppressed adolescent fantasies—very much unconstrained in young boys—of violence, energy, revenge, or transgression. But this occurs also, don't forget, at the hands of the hero. In these works the moral *alter ego* of Batman is Gordon, the police chief, not the Joker. The villain must be utterly repulsive and crepuscular . . . yet this opens up the "dangerous" notion of justified revenge on behalf of the illiberal masses. Given their lowness as a form, comics can luxuriate in the "badness" of the hero—even to the point of pitilessness.

For example, the pulp magazine from the '30s, *The Shadow*, that Batman slightly resembles, luxuriated in vigilantism, sadism, punishment of criminals, and revenge by one's fireside. The radio show based on it was the most listened to in America at that time. Orson Welles played the virtual anti-hero.

Anyway, by the comic's conclusion, Batman, Slade, and the Joker are in their rightful places. It is all revealed to have been a plot to assassinate Batman in a disused canal lock. The Joker and Slade are accomplices. They are cold-blooded psychopaths. Batman is their eternal enemy. Yet he turns the tables on them, escapes from underwater, kicks Slade unconscious, and pursues the Joker towards the sports car: the Batmobile. The man who smiles without mirth can't start it and is beaten by the Avenger, but, under the Code, a moral ending must be enforced. All collaboration is spent. Batman overcomes his desire to enact an extra-juridical killing. The Joker will be returned to a state correctional institution for the criminally insane, Arkham Asylum.

Nonetheless, for a brief moment the Joker and Batman were on the same side against Gordon (and Slade), prior to the inevitable reversal. The idea remains notwithstanding that the dramaturgy between these characters can become more complex—if adult psychology and philosophy is added. Finally, such a comic (virtually forgotten now and a third of a century old) exemplifies the *naked fascism of the heroic avenger* up to the penultimate frame.

Counter-Currents/*North American New Right*
November 14, 2010

ARKHAM ASYLUM:
AN ANALYSIS

JONATHAN BOWDEN

Arkham Asylum: A Serious House on Serious Earth
Story by Grant Morrison, art by Dave McKean
New York: DC Comics, 1989

 Arkham Asylum claims to be among the most "adult" comics ever produced, and, although there are a few other candidates, it does merit this accolade up to a point. It has also inspired numerous spinoffs, including video games. Elsewhere I have written about a Batman and the Joker team-up comic from the mid-seventies, but this was deliberately circumscribed by the Comics Code Authority and lacked a mature sensibility.
 Note: By "adult," I am not referring to a predilection for transgression, low-grade, or "edgy" material here. Most of these attempts in popular culture are faintly ludicrous, it has to be said. No. What I am referring to is transgression of the philosophical limitations placed on such narratives by an insistent Dualism. This leads to a totally uncomplicated schema where the forces of light and darkness ply their trade in a Manichean way.
 The first point of departure is in the treatment of mental illness. Nearly all of the villains in this institution for the criminally insane are regarded (by the storyline) as mad, bad, and dangerous to know. They are all considered to be responsible for their actions irrespective of their madness. In this respect, Arkham—in a fictionalized New York City called Gotham—resembles a British mental hospital such as Broadmoor. This establishment was erected in Berkshire in the 1850s as the prototypical insti-

tution for the criminally insane—even though such descriptions are studiously avoided.

All of the super-villains contained herein—the Joker, Two-Face, Croc, Black-mask, Doctor Destiny, the Mad Hatter, the Scarecrow, Clay Face, Maxie Zeus, Tweedle-Dum and Tweedle-Dee, Professor Milo, etc.—are held to be accountable for their crimes, but treatable. This accords with the liberal-humanist notion (based on Pelagianism) that Man is naturally good, rational, kind, humane, and non-criminal. The facts of Man's post-animalian state completely militate against this, of course, but don't forget that we're dealing with an ideology here.

Several psychotherapists are employed in the institution in order to treat the maniacs contained therein. When the lunatics take over the asylum (quite literally), some of them even volunteer to remain with their charges. They have a responsibility, you see.

Just like in a real hospital, a range of treatments (whether medical or ideological) is tried: paint-spot/Rorschach tests, word association mind-games, as well as classic Freudianism—whereas some of the other "therapies" are obviously from the Behavioral school. The director of the institution even uses severe ECT (Electro-Convulsive Therapy) on the "patients." This is interesting for two reasons: one, the anti-psychiatric movement campaigned against this from the 1960s onwards; and, two, it indicates the biological basis of mental illness. It can only be physically assailed if it is somatic to begin with.

In fact, those who are criminally insane fall into two large categories. The offences that they commit—murder, rape, cannibalism, etc.—tend to be rather similar, but the originating conditions are very distinct. The two categories are psychopathia and schizophrenia. Interestingly, the word psychopath (reduced to "psycho" in popular language) is now deeply "offensive" or politically incorrect. It has got to the point that certain staff in these hospitals can be disciplined if they make use of it.

Psychopathia is a birth condition—that is, persons suffering from an advanced personality disorder are born and not made. Psychopaths begin torturing animals about age of four to six and then proceed onto young children later. They regard killing their own species as the equivalent of swatting a fly. Likewise, for them rape is normal sex. It appears that psychopaths are hard-wired to believe that life happens to be a constant war zone of each against all ... and that love is hatred, quite literally.

They are relatively incapable of lying, unlike normal humans who are mendacious all the time. (Note: this is usually to survive social situations without conflict.) Psychopaths live for conflict, believe life to be worthless, and have utter contempt for social workers, parole board types, concerned professors, and do-gooders who attempt to help them. They often advocate the harshest punishments for criminals of their sort (excluding possibly themselves); they would love to apply such indignities with the maximum amount of torture or humiliation. Psychopaths lack certain female chromosomes (if male) which soften the ferocity of the male nature and prepare it for camaraderie, fatherhood, paternalism, and the softer virtues.

One of the most famous psychopaths in criminology was Peter Kürten (the basis for Fritz Lang's film *M*) who was executed in Germany in the early 1930s. This occurred during that authoritarian halfway house period (typified by a whiff of Conservative Revolutionism) between the end of Weimar and Hitler's rise.

The Joker is certainly a psychopath, but in *Arkham Asylum* he is presented as suffering from Tourette's syndrome. This is a clever notion, because Tourette's is a complicated diagnosis with both positive and negative characteristics. (Mozart is believed to have suffered from it, for instance.) The simplistic thing to say is that Tourette's is a tic-based condition which is both genetic and inherited (i.e., strictly biological). The Joker's mindless and repetitive desire to be rude, upset social order, utter blasphemies, and be mentally sadistic (whilst grinning inanely) are all part and parcel of it.

Yet, if we probe deeper, the Joker can also be diagnosed as suffering from Super Sanity: his ego is completely suppressed, and experience washes over him continuously. He has no filter in relation to hyper-reality (in other words) and is therefore incapable of a conservative gesture, whether linguistically, morally, violently, sexually, etc. Everything is in the moment—he is a pure Existentialist without remit or prior expectancy. With him, Being is becoming—to use philosophical language.

He bears a strong resemblance—as a result of this—to the personality of Caligula, the mad Roman emperor, as designated in Robert Graves' *I, Claudius* and *Claudius the God*, as well as Albert Camus' absurdist play. To bring it to a point: the Joker, like the Mad God Caligula, can embrace you, flirt with you, assassinate you, and dance with the corpse—while laughing continuously . . . as well as having tears of mock-genuine sadness flowing down his cheeks. "I've done away with my best friend, but he deserved it" would be a typical remark.

Batman, by point of contrast, is everything which is ordered, finite, prior, Right-wing, *a priori*, anti-atheistic (in a metaphysical sense), and Objective . . . philosophically. Bruce Wayne (Batman) is a metaphysical Objectivist, a Fascist; the Joker (by dint of contrast) is an anarchist. Yet anarchism and fascism are tied together by virtue of their dialectical inversions of one another. Scratch Nietzsche and you move to Stirner (in the center of this spectrum); scratch Stirner and you end up with the individualistic element in Bakunin, for example. You can also go back along the spectrum as well.

Another consideration arises: the notion of the anarcho-fascist or Right-wing anarchist (a combination of

Batman and the Joker). This would include a great number of artists, such as Céline, D. H. Lawrence, Wyndham Lewis, Gottfried Benn, Ernst Jünger, Yukio Mishima, Drieu La Rochelle, T. E. Lawrence, Ezra Pound, and so forth. A new conundrum also arises here: most far-Right leaders (unlike the majority of their followers) exhibit Anarch traits, the most notorious political artist of the 20th century being Adolf Hitler, of course. (Note: the supporters of such movements tend to be much more conservative than their leaders, *per se*; they look to such individuals to provide the rebellious conformism, aggressive normalcy, and transgressive stoicism that the Right needs.)

But if we might return to *Arkham Asylum* proper: one of the other major tropes is the treatment of homosexuality. Interestingly, the writer, a Scottish creator called Grant Morrison, wished to visualize the Joker as an effeminate (if threatening) transvestite replete with French bodice and underwear. This is to accentuate the grinning red lips, green hair, palsied or blanched skin, string tie, purple jacket and slacks, and green dress shirt of the original. To link inversion with a psychopathic clown (i.e., a negative image) is relatively reckless on Morrison's part . . . given that any such treatment would be considered "politically incorrect."

In Italian neorealist cinema after the Second World War (for instance) two lesbians were used as a dark or sinister portrayal of fascism, but negative depictions of inversion are rare in contemporary media. (This is contrary to the liberal-Left view that "homophobia" lurks as an omnipresent catch-all.) The last sinister depiction which I can recall is the triumvirate of villains in the Humphrey Bogart version of *The Maltese Falcon*. This starred, quite memorably, Sidney Greenstreet as the eponymous Fat Man. I remember a bourgeois Marxist catalog from the 1980s at the National Film Theatre (in Britain) describing the villainous troupe's portrayal as an example of "bigotry."

Nonetheless, Morrison's schemata for the Joker continues—with him embodying an inverted sadism in contrast to Batman's gruff, no-nonsense, Josef Thorak-laced, and straight as an arrow sensibility.

There are also some terrific scenes in this *folie à deux* (so to say); one of which occurs at the end of the piece. In this particular, Batman starts wrecking the asylum with an axe, and, as he does so, one of the maniacs runs down various corridors (in this Bedlamite labyrinth, you understand) screaming "the Bat—the Bat; he's destroying *everything!*" To which Black-mask responds, "You see, Joker; he's too powerful, you should never have let him in here."

In a great panel, drawn and painted by Dave McKean, the Joker screams as a false martyr: "That's it! Go on, blame me, go on . . . do!" All of this is accompanied by the quiff of emerald hair and the manic smile—amid tons of greasepaint—which just grins on and on without mirth. Just how far the author, Morrison, is aware of any symmetry with Otto Weininger's *Sex and Character* is a moot point, however. In his own mind, he is probably trying to create the "wildest" version of Batman on record, nothing more.

In finality, *Arkham Asylum* goes quite a long way towards considering Batman as a putative Superman (in a Nietzschean sense). First of all, he has to overcome distaste at going in the place to begin with; then he must confront his own "demons"—by virtue of the mentally questionable state of someone who dresses up as a bat in order to beat up criminals for a living. Also, Batman seems hesitant in the face of the Joker's triumphant lunacy inside the Asylum where he can posture as the Lord of Misrule. In one revealing moment he refers to an Arkham run by lunatics as the "real world." Presumably, in this context, the world outside the gates superintended by Commissioner Gordon is unreal.

Nevertheless, Batman goes through a series of tests—

even a crucifixion *manqué*—as he gradually conquers the place and subdues it to his will. Over time he sidesteps Harvey Dent's (Two-Face's) deconstruction from dualism, beats down upon Clayface's disease, refuses the nightmares of Doctor Destiny, or the serendipity of Professor Milo. Likewise, he emerges from the Scarecrow's cell unscathed and confronts the man-alligator, Croc, in a clash of the Titans. Yet, throughout the whole process, he is getting stronger and stronger . . . as he engages in personal transcendence or self-over-becoming. Until, by the end of this film on paper, he can absorb the insanity of the place, sublimate it, purge it, throw it forward, and then clamber out on top of it.

By the time the drama ends, Batman makes a move to rejoin the waiting police (headed by Gordon) and the media outside. The criminal lunatics remain inside where they belong, but in a strangely subdued way. The fascistic hero may have lanced the boil (granted), but he has only been able to do so by reintegration, fanaticism for a cause outside oneself, and the adoption of a strength greater than reason. At the end (although sane) he has incorporated part of the Joker's Tarot (The Fool or The Hanged Man) into his own purview.

To use an Odinic or pagan device, he is walking with Weird or embracing his own Destiny (fate)—i.e., the will which lies at the end of the road where you will the end's refusal. In this state—perhaps—a fictionalized variant on the end of the Charlemagne Division exists. Remember: they fought on to the end in a fire-torn Berlin because they had no country of their own to return to.

It is intriguing to point out the states which a form of entertainment for children can begin to approach. But it's only a funny book, isn't it?

Counter-Currents/*North American New Right*,
December 31, 2010

BATMAN AS COMEDY

SPENCER J. QUINN

Other than with the campy television program from the 1960s, you're probably not going to equate Batman very often with comedy.

Of course, there is ample room for dark humor in Batman stories. *The Killing Joke* by Alan Moore is great example. But this is not the same thing as comedy, in which the universe itself is funny. With Batman, the universe is more twisted than anything else. It's always high noon in the middle of the night with the forces of abject evil baying like ravenous hyenas, waiting for civilization to weaken and stumble. All that we've worked for is beset on all sides by corruption and barbarism and apathy, and is always a knife's edge away from pure anarchy. That's why need vigilant heroes like the Batman as a bulwark against our greatest fears.

Over the top just a wee tad? Sure. But we love it anyway.

While most superhero comic books recognize Good and Evil, Batman stories tend to have a more Right-wing appeal for the way they identify this evil. For Batman, evil is not highbrow so much as it is base, brutish, and nasty. Superman may zoom through the heavens to thwart Lex Luthor's latest ingenious scheme or defend Earth from some intergalactic predator. But Batman is the one getting his knuckles bloody as he beats mafia henchmen to a pulp. Unlike most other heroes, Batman must stoop to face evil as if it were vermin. And the deranged, in the Batman world, may as well be vermin. Notice how Batman's villains are all caricatures of the insane: Joker, Riddler, Penguin. They don't even have super powers. They're just stark raving mad and obsessively diabolical. Batman has to deal with hideous people like this. And he is only a man, so it all takes effort.

A more Left-wing approach would be for the hero to "punch-up" (to borrow a phrase from *Doonesbury*'s Garry Trudeau). In such a milieu, the wealthy and powerful are the root of all evil since they are most often blamed for greatest Left-wing evil of them all: inequality. A true Left-winger's heart bleeds for the downtrodden, the poor, the underdog. Such a hero may have to deal with trouble on the street, but more often than not, it is the respectable, beautiful elites lurking in their mansions with bags of money who are the real culprits. Look to the Spirit, another urban crime fighter, who is a little more along these lines than Batman is. In any case, since inequality among humans is inescapable, evil in a Left-wing world must be permanent.

For the Right-wing, evil is not some socioeconomic construct to be eliminated by progress, but something that lies in the hearts of all men. Batman has it too, and that is why we love him. He contains it, he overcomes it. This is a struggle we all have to face. Further, because he has intimate knowledge of evil, he knows that we must be ruthless when fighting it. You must stamp evil out, or it will consume everything. I'll even go so far as to say that most Right-wingers have a little id-like Batman living inside their minds, itching to bust heads. Where a Left-winger may feel compassion for the deranged and seek a cure, Right-wingers will more likely see monsters in human form who must be stopped, one way or another. Where a Left-winger would prefer to send a thief to prison for rehabilitation, a Right-winger would wish he could cut the thief's hand off.

And this is very real.

I'm reminded of a story the great Iowa wrestler Dan Gable relates about his sister, who was raped and murdered in the 1960s when he was still in high school. As Gable tells it, he made himself obsessed with wrestling in order to take his parents' minds off their all-consuming grief. He obliterated everyone in his weight division and won the state tournament, but it didn't matter. His parents' couldn't let go. Every day, Gable's father would take an unloaded rifle to a hill near the prison and wait for the convicts to be let out into the yard. Then he would find the man who murdered his daughter, take aim, and fire. And fire. And fire.

Remember that Bruce Wayne's parents were also murdered in cold blood, and the boy responded in an eerily similar way. If there is one word to describe such a reaction, it is "healthy." It is the ardent desire to never let evil out of your sights, and to fire and fire and fire. That is essentially what Batman is all about.

Yet, if evil can be stamped out or contained in Batman's Right-wing urban purgatory, then a world without evil could theoretically exist. What then? Well, this is where comedy comes in.

Batman in a world without evil is . . . believe it or not . . . funny.

By funny, I don't mean black comedy or satire. I'm thinking more along the lines of Benny Hill or the Keystone Cops minus all the sped-up motion. This precious concept is best illustrated by my all-time favorite Batman story which appeared in Detective Comics Issue 567 in October 1986. It's entitled, "The Night of Thanks, but no Thanks!" It's a one-shot story written by none other than Harlan Ellison. And it is hysterical.

(Spoiler alert)

It's shortly after midnight, and we find Batman about to swoop down upon a convenience store robbery. But when he arrives, the proprietor puts a gun to the thief's head and tells Batman to find a payphone and call 911. Grudgingly, Batman does so.

Half an hour later, Batman spots a mugging in progress, a man trying to rob a lady. Our masked hero then rushes to the lady's aid only to find her now beating the crap out of the mugger, Ruth Buzzi-style, with her purse. She then *orders* Batman to make himself useful and call a cop. Next we see ol' Bats back on the phone saying, "Yeah, it's me again. Wanna make something of it?"

So, you see where this is going. Batman finds a crisis, and either he is not the one to solve it, or he discovers it's not really a crisis, or he actually makes matters worse. A young man is about to jump off a ledge, but before Batman can make his cinematic rescue, a cop reaches through a window and beats him to it. Batman finds someone trying to break into a car only to discover that it is the car's owner who had locked his keys inside. Batman busts a drug deal and then learns that he had just blown the careful ruse of an undercover cop. He then sees someone on a ladder disabling a security alarm. Turns out it's a technician who is innocently fixing it. She then asks Batman to hold her flashlight while she works and gripes when he doesn't hold it steadily enough.

At 2:16 am, Batman is sitting on a park bench feeling sorry for himself and doing nothing. In what other story are you going to find Batman sitting on a park bench feeling sorry for himself and doing nothing?

Finally, 3:54, he spots an actual crime. A big, baldheaded brute coming his way eating a candy bar. The man has the nerve to toss the wrapper onto the pavement. Batman stands heroically in this criminal's way and gets on his case for littering.

Yes, the great Batman, reduced to fighting the dreaded crime of littering.

And just when you think the Caped Crusader may actually have a fight on his hands, the gentleman concedes the argument as eloquently as possible. He picks up the wrapper and tosses in it a trash can, all the while apologizing profusely and thanking Batman for reinforcing good citizenship. He walks away wishing Batman the very thing he wants the least: a quiet evening.

The story ends at 4:16 am with Bruce Wayne's butler Alfred discovering Bruce sulking in his study. "Master Bruce!" the old man says, "Your patrol ended early. Was it a trying evening filled with the usual danger, sir?"

"Worst night of my life, Alfred," a despondent Bruce responds. "Absolutely, without a doubt, the most miserable night of my life."

Reflecting on the Batman-as-comedy idea, I believe, may teach folks on the Right the greatest lesson about fighting evil. It really is about the destination and not the journey. Fighting for fighting's sake is, for lack of a better term, bad. Evil *can* be stamped out or contained. That is the very purpose of our forming great civilizations. And once we get to that point, we should know to tone down the fighting to appropriate levels. We should know to relax a little and *enjoy* our lives. Unlike the Left which will never stop fighting for a utopia that can never be achieved, we on the Right understand that life doesn't have to be a constant struggle, and it doesn't have to be perfect. There will be nights when things take care of themselves just fine. And we should be thankful for that.

But if we take the fighting evil idea too close to heart, it becomes more about the former and less about the latter. When that happens, we'll end up just like Batman, haunting a peaceful city and wishing desperately for war.

Only then it won't be quite so funny.

Counter-Currents/*North American New Right*,
May 29, 2018

TIM BURTON'S BATMAN:
PUTTING THE GOTHIC INTO GOTHAM

DAVID YORKSHIRE

ORIGINS & EVOLUTION OF THE GOTHIC IN FILM
The gothic is a quintessentially European aesthetic. Moreover, it pertains and appeals more specifically to those of North-West European descent and is to be found in various modes and tropes throughout North-West European culture and contrasts with the Classicism of Southern Europe. Gothic as a term was first applied to medieval art and particularly architecture by Renaissance critics in similar propagandist fashion to how the term Dark Ages was also used to describe the period following the collapse of the Roman Empire. In both cases, the terms were coined to denigrate Germanic ascendancy in culture as unenlightened and barbaric in relation to the culture of Greco-Roman Classical Antiquity and its Renaissance.[1]

Equally, when the Gothic appeared in literature towards the end of the 18th century, it was as a reaction to Enlightenment Classicism and the Age of Reason. Gothic motifs here are typically old aristocratic families, subterranean and eerie settings, the past—particularly the medieval past—entering the present, the supernatural, emo-

---

[1] See Giorgio Vasari, *The Lives of the Artists*, trans. J. C. and P. Bondanella (Oxford: Oxford University Press, 1991), pp. 117, 527, and Giorgio Vasari in *Vasari on Technique: Being the Introduction to the Three Arts of Design, Architecture, Sculpture and Painting, Prefixed to the Lives of the Most Excellent Painters, Sculptors and Architects*, ed. G. Baldwin Brown, trans. Louisa S. Maclehose (London: Dent, 1907), 83ff.

tional extremes in characterization, an older powerful antagonist, a young hero, and a heroine that faces some sort of imprisonment or constraint. As regards the subterranean and eerie settings, typical are those again often associated with the medieval: dungeons, castles, manor houses, churches, and cathedrals.[2]

Contemporary (read post-Marxian) critical theory relating to the Gothic has centered on the subject of transgression against societal norms, yet what is rarely addressed is that these norms are post-Enlightenment, not meaning from the likes of Kant or Franklin, but from the radical liberal tradition beginning with Locke. In other words, the transgressive forces of the Gothic proper (as opposed to contemporary texts that often attempt to subvert the genre itself) are not those compatible with any philosophical position further Left, but, in their traditional and mythical rootedness in what is quintessentially European, can only honestly be interpreted from the Right. While the old liberal radical Left used the term Gothic disparagingly,[3] the New Left of the post-1960s cultural revolution has appropriated the Gothic for its countercultural impact, while either critiquing or attempting to divorce it from its Rightist elements, such as those pertaining to aristocracy, myth, religiosity, and Eurocentrism.

In this struggle between the rationality of the Enlightenment and the alleged unreason of the Gothic, one can see a foreshadowing of the philosophies to come that relate to the human condition: the persona and shadow of Jung and the Apollonian and Dionysian of Nietzsche, the "darker" aspects in both philosophies being defined in re-

---

[2] For more on the subject, see for example, David Punter, *The Gothic* (London: John Wiley & Sons, 2004).

[3] See Fred Botting, "In Gothic Darkly: Heterotopia, History Culture" in *A Companion to the Gothic*, ed. David Punter (Oxford: Blackwell, 2000), 3–14.

lation to post-Enlightenment bourgeois society. Yet with both of these philosophies, one sees a reconciliation of polarities beyond good and evil.

The Gothic as a genre in and of itself has all but disappeared and is often referred in post-Gothic texts as "the Gothic mode," diffused as it is throughout other genres. In film, one sees it readily in German Expressionism, in its Hollywood derivative Film Noir, and in more contemporary genres like Steampunk. Here, cinematic settings in particular are atmospherically Gothic: the urban cityscapes are often eerily lonely and dark, often nocturnal, and the characters that inhabit them psychologically extreme. German Expressionism exaggerates the *mise en scène* to reflect a psychological imbalance in characters; the architecture is therefore often stylistically Gothic, as the form lends to this extremity. Steampunk's reinterpretation and advancement of Victorianism into the present, often creating alternate timelines where the digital revolution never occurred and steam remained the basis of technology, inevitably bring with them the high Victorian architectural style of the Neo-Gothic.

Steampunk was certainly influenced by events in the world of distinctly white European forms of music. The rise of industrial, gothic rock, and darker new wave bands like the Damned, the Cure, Bauhaus, and the Sisters of Mercy, to name the more famous ones, created a whole new post-punk aesthetic, in which its acolytes wore black, especially leather and plastic clothing, white make-up, and silver jewelry. The aesthetic had a distinct Victorian vampiric look to it, and it was no surprise that its adherents were called simply Goths. The music videos that accompanied the singles released into the charts were set in the city back alleys at the junction of Film Noir and Steampunk. Although this cultural scene began in part, perhaps appropriately, in the industrial yet culturally traditionalist north of England, its Mecca was to be found in the metropolis of London, in a nightclub named the Batcave.

ORIGINS OF THE GOTHIC IN BATMAN

Batman was originally set in New York City. According to Batman's co-creator Bob Kane, the name Gotham came quite by chance:

> Originally I was going to call Gotham City "Civic City." Then I tried "Capital City," then "Coast City." Then I flipped through the New York City phone book and spotted the name "Gotham Jewelers" and said, "That's it," Gotham City. We didn't call it New York because we wanted anybody in any city to identify with it.[4]

Gotham is an antiquated nickname for the Big Apple, and its appearance in the telephone directory was as incidental as its selection was not. The name Gotham was coined by Washington Irving (and one notes his connection to the Gothic literary mode) in 1807 and taken from the village of Gotham in Nottinghamshire, England, a village notable for its habitation by fools. This cannot have been far from both Kane and writer Bill Finger's mind when creating a lawless city inhabited by crazy villains, and, whether consciously or subconsciously, neither can Gotham's phonemic association with the Gothic.

In spite of Kane and Finger's ethnicity that often inclines members of their tribe to be at odds with Western culture, they created a character that is very much in the European tradition. The character of Batman himself is a hybrid of both the Classical and the Gothic. Kane stated that the idea for his form came from a design for an orni-

---

[4] Cited in Jim Steranko, *The Steranko History of Comics* (Reading, Penn.: Supergraphics, 1970), 44.

thopter flying machine by Leonardo Da Vinci with the inscription "Remember that your bird shall have no other model than the bat."[5] Yet the shadowy chiropteran costume is equally Gothic, as are Batman's nocturnal habits, which all serve to bring to mind that archetype of Gothic literature: the vampire.

The outward vestments of Batman and his alter-ego Bruce Wayne serve to reveal the inner compartmentalization of two major character aspects to the audience. Wayne's bourgeois suit emphasizes the modern Renaissance man, the Apollonian persona constructed for polite society, "persona" of course meaning both character and mask. Ignoring the camp 1960s television series version, the Batsuit's Gothic external mask disguises the Dionysian shadow within.

Indeed, the 1960s series did much to undo Batman's Gothic image, which only really recovered thanks to Frank Miller's *Dark Knight* series of comic books from the late 1980s. Indeed, it was Miller's success in reinvigorating the comic character that led directly to interest in a potential film. It is, however, perhaps quite ironic that Christopher Nolan's Dark Knight Trilogy has concentrated more on gritty realism than a stylized Gothicism, although this may also have been a conscious decision not to attempt to recreate the Tim Burton films.[6]

TIM BURTON & GOTHIC BATMAN

In addition to Miller's graphic reinterpretation of Batman, one other event enabled the filming of 1989's *Bat-*

---

[5] Interview with Bob Kane, *The Two Masks of the Caped Crusader*, The Family Channel, 1990.

[6] Christopher Sharrett, "Batman and the Twilight of the Idols: An Interview with Frank Miller" in *The Many Lives of Batman: Critical Approaches to a Superhero and his Media*, ed. Roberta E. Pearson and William Uricchio (New York: Routledge, 1991), 33–46.

man: Richard Donner's 1978 version of *Superman*, hailed as the first modern superhero film. In the cinematic superhero overload of today, it is difficult to comprehend the impact the film had, or to imagine a prior cultural space in which a serious filmic treatment of a superhero was seen as a daring move. Indeed, Donner's original grossed far more at the box office than any of its campier and cornier sequels.

The aforementioned genres of German Expressionism, Film Noir, and Steampunk contract to a point in *Batman*. Gotham's criminals and police are attired in the 1940s suits of Film Noir that are by no means out of place in their surroundings. The cityscape of Gotham itself is an aesthetic blend of Steampunk with Film Noir. The art deco theatres and gothic tenement blocks are juxtaposed with fantastic Steampunk appendages: pumps, pipes, vents, shafts, fans, and ducts, which constantly belch out steam. The Steampunk setting culminates in crime boss Carl Grissom's chemical plant, and it is no coincidence that this building is where the (il)logic of comic book fantasy overrides the laws of physics, Jack Napier plummeting into a vat of chemicals and being transformed into the Joker.

The Steampunk settings are also congruent with German Expressionist cinema, and there are obvious nods to Fritz Lang's *Metropolis*. The high altitudes and odd angles of both building construction and civil engineering within the film and camerawork as creative process of the film reveal the huge influence of German Expressionism and also correspond nicely to the demands of a film in which the main character emulates the aerial swoops of the bat. The film is replete with downward and upward shots that give the audience a collective sense of vertigo that destabilizes the equilibrium of the senses and transports it beyond its comfortable bourgeois world of safety and reason.

It is no coincidence that the film ends with multiple

opportunities for these vertical shots as Batman fights the Joker, rescuing Vicki Vale from him in a Gothic cathedral, high up in the belfry and above the ribbed vaults and flying buttresses and onto the roof, in almost a re-enactment of the climactic scene in *Metropolis* in which Freder Fredersen rescues Maria from the mad scientist Rotwang. Indeed, one can readily see similarities between the Joker and Rotwang in their insanity, scientific expertise, and narrative functions in the two films.

Where the two characters differ most significantly is in their respective relationships to modernity and tradition. Rotwang bears the greater similarity to the "mad professor" archetype of Gothic fiction, for there is no rejection of prior cultural tradition. The Joker's vandalism in the museum as he abducts Vicki Vale is an attack on traditional and bourgeois culture; Rembrandts, Degas, Renoirs, Gainsboroughs are all defaced, while the piece by Francis Bacon is left intact: "I kinda like this one, Bob. Leave it." He represents the Left-wing anarchist, whose only aim is to destroy America as a cultural extension of Europe.

Many fans have criticized the use of the pop singer Prince's songs in the film, yet one notes the context in their employment; they invariably accompany the Joker on his "artistic" and "theatrical" endeavors—here in his deconstruction of traditional art and also during his gaudy lowbrow parade. In its Negroid superficiality, Prince's music fits the bill perfectly.

In contradistinction, accompanying Batman/Wayne is the classical film score by Danny Elfman. Both the Bruce Wayne and Batman identities come from quintessentially European traditions in their construction by Burton and company, the bourgeois Classicism of Bruce Wayne and the reconfigured Gothic Batman for the postmodern technological age being split into a very dualist Apollonian persona and Dionysian shadow, as is revealed in the dinner scene between Bruce Wayne and Vicki Vale, when

Wayne, uncomfortable as Vale in the vast Gothic dining hall, suggests they go into the kitchen:

> **VICKI VALE:** You know, this house and all this stuff really doesn't seem like you at all.
> **BRUCE WAYNE:** Some of it is very much me, and some of it isn't.
> **VICKI VALE:** That dining room is definitely not you.
> **BRUCE WAYNE:** No, the dining room isn't.

The Gothic dining room is not Wayne, but it is Batman, as is, ironically, the whole Gothic edifice of Wayne Manor, underneath which the equally Gothic (in terms of narrative mode rather than architectural style) Batcave is hidden, revealing that Batman is Wayne's *Dasein* and Wayne a mere social actor. The Jungian shadow is therefore the true self and the persona, as its etymology suggests, a mere mask.

When Wayne leaves the dining room with Vale, it is because being with Vale in the room makes him uncomfortable. He is awkward in conversation and table manners, and it is Vale who reveals the inappropriateness of the room by exaggerating her mannerisms as she puts her hand to the side of her mouth and calls to Wayne at the other end of the long table. The acting by the male and female leads is commendable, with Michael Keaton's awkwardness juxtaposing well with Kim Basinger's self-assuredness in bourgeois society. What Wayne represents is very much the aristocrat awkwardly attempting to fit into a society now ruled and modelled by the bourgeoisie.

Here we have then an interesting morality at the center of Burton's *Batman*. Whether consciously or subconsciously—and one notes Burton's unconscious attraction to the Gothic—we are served a critique of bourgeois superficiality and the society of manners and mannerisms as anathema to the heroic. Furthermore, these social conventions are seen as distinctly feminine, the gendered self-assuredness being reversed when these conventions are broken by those who operate outside them, like the Joker. Suddenly, Vale becomes the helpless damsel in distress of Gothic fiction, and Wayne assumes his natural role as Gothic hero, and it is no coincidence that the Joker is (literally) brought down in the finale by a gargoyle from the aforementioned Gothic cathedral.

Burton's attraction to the Gothic as a white European has then resulted in both his subversion and masculinizing of the mode, as he recreates it in his own image. In the Gothic literary genre proper, it is the villain who is the personification of the "True Rightist" traditional and mythic past—a representation of the superstition and barbarity of particularly the so-called "Dark Ages." Yet in Batman, we have a "Dark Enlightenment," where the post-Enlightenment Apollonian bourgeois world can only be saved from the forces of nihilism by a Dionysian *Übermensch* who embraces pre-Enlightenment ideals of aristocratic paternalism, the warrior code, an appreciation of the mythic and tradition—ideals that are subverted in true Gothic texts like Bram Stoker's *Dracula* or Ann Radcliffe's *The Mysteries of Udolpho*. As Jonathan Bowden often pointed out, this is ever the irony in Hollywood's masculine archetype: that the aristocratic warrior type must always defend the liberal capitalism of the bourgeoisified West.

In all, Burton has created a filmic extravaganza specifically tailored to the sensibilities of the white European male. The only significant Black character in the film is that of the reconfigured Harvey Dent. The decision to cast a black American actor in Billy Dee Williams as a canonically white character was a conscious one on Burton's part as he looked ahead to Dent's becoming the villain Two Face. He was interested in the black and white concept. What he meant or where he was going with that was never realized.⁷ Critics like Camille Bacon-Smith and Tyrone Yarbrough have attempted to prove that as many blacks attended *Batman* showings as whites, based upon a cursory head count at single showings at a tiny sample of picture houses,⁸ but the hype surrounding the film was well-documented at the time, and audiences were overwhelmingly white. Her study shows rather the dishonesty of contemporary academia.

The film, then, is a white film for white audiences. Tim Burton's version of the Batman narrative is not merely a retelling of Batman, but simultaneously, a postmodern retelling of the Gothic tale, which in turn, is a retelling of European folktale and fairytale. Certainly, Burton's ever expanding portfolio of work bears out this assertion, and, in spite of restraints, constraints, and conventions imposed upon the film industry by both Hollywood's Jewish executives and the state apparatus with regard to the employment of ethnic minorities, Burton's films remain firmly in the European artistic tradition.

Counter-Currents/North American New Right,
July 20, 2016

---

⁷ Tim Burton, "Commentary," *Batman Special Edition*, PolyGram/Warner Bros., 2005.

⁸ Camilla Bacon-Smith and Tyrone Yarbrough, "Batman: The Ethnography" in *The Many Lives of Batman*, 90–116.

BATMAN RETURNS:
AN ANTI-SEMITIC ALLEGORY?

ANDREW HAMILTON

Soon after the release of director Tim Burton's *Batman Returns* (1992) starring Michael Keaton as Batman, Danny DeVito as the Penguin, Michelle Pfeiffer as Catwoman, and Christopher Walken as evil capitalist Max Shreck, America's premier newspaper, the Jewish-controlled *New York Times*, published an op-ed piece by two Columbia College seniors, Rebecca Roiphe and Daniel Cooper, entitled "Batman and the Jewish Question" (July 2, 1992).

Today, Roiphe, the daughter of feminist Anne Roiphe, is a professor at New York Law School.

Batman Returns is the second movie in the series, after Tim Burton's inaugural *Batman* (1989). It told the tale of the Penguin, a freakish villain who posed a deadly threat to the citizens of Gotham City. As a deformed baby, he had been secretly set adrift *à la* Moses in Gotham City's river by his parents, who deemed him repellant.

Nurtured in the sewers, the Penguin tries to seize political control of the metropolis with the help of wealthy, megalomaniacal industrialist Max Shreck. Ultimately, the Penguin mounts an attack to kidnap and murder all of the first-born aristocratic children of Gotham City.

This last plot element, an obvious reference to Passover, was introduced by Jewish screenwriter Wesley Strick, who admitted, "Of course I was referring to Exodus."[1]

In their article, the two Ivy League Jews charged that

---

[1] http://www.nytimes.com/1992/07/20/opinion/l-anti-semitism-in-batman-returns-be-serious-who-s-really-divisive-122392.html

Batman Returns was anti-Semitic. The Penguin, they averred, "is not just a deformed man, half human, half-Arctic-beast. He is a Jew, down to his hooked nose, pale face, and lust for herring."

Some of Roiphe's and Cooper's allegations make little sense to a non-Jew.

For example: the Penguin's "umbrellas that transform into bayonets, machine guns, and helicopters are Moses' magic staff. The flipper hands he holds at his chest are Moses' hands, which in Exodus become 'leprous as snow.'" The Penguin's "army of mindless followers, a flock of ineffectual birds who cannot fly, is eventually converted to the side of Christian morality. They turn against the leader who has failed to assimilate."

One could deconstruct their argument further, but my objective here is to report Jewish perceptions.

Here were some of their charges:

- Using "images and cultural stereotypes," director Tim Burton "depicts the Penguin as one of the oldest cultural clichés: the Jew who is bitter, bent over, and out for revenge, the Jew who is unathletic and seemingly unthreatening but who, in fact, wants to murder every firstborn child of the gentile community."
- "The Penguin feigns assimilation into society and gains the citizens' trust for a time. But eventually even the ignorant masses understand this false prophet for what he is, a primordial beast who seeks retribution, 'an eye for an eye.'"
- The evil, wealthy capitalist who allies himself with the Penguin against the citizens of Gotham is named "Max Shreck" after German actor Max Schreck, who portrayed Dracula in F. W. Murnau's Expressionist silent film classic, *Nosferatu* (1922). Metaphorically, Shreck is a blood-sucking vampire.

- The Gentile Shreck "wants only power, but the Jew who has suffered wants to punish others for the crime that was committed against him."
- "The Penguin's evil plan is the enactment of a paranoid notion that Jews' effort to preserve their heritage and culture is a guise for elitist and hostile intentions."
- "*Batman Returns* takes place at Christmas time. The Christmas tree, the lights and the mistletoe serve a thematic purpose. They represent the Christian ethic, which will save Gotham City from the false ideology of the Penguin. In the final scene Batman articulates the distinctly Christian moral of this film: 'Merry Christmas and good will toward men . . . and women.'"
- Finally, the authors discern a Wagnerian motif: Jewish composer Danny Elfman's musical score, they say, "makes indisputable the influence of Richard Wagner." In addition, director Burton's horde of penguins are like the Niebelungen; the "Penguin-Jew-villain" is Wagner's Alberich from *Das Rheingold*; and the duck-shaped boat in which the Penguin navigates Gotham's sewers is a parody of the "Schwan der Scheldt" from *Lohengrin*.

THE CHORUS CHIMES IN

Publication of these accusations in the *Times* conferred instant legitimacy upon them. The article generated numerous letters to the editor, commentaries in other venues, and was republished across the country. One large metropolitan daily re-ran it under the headline "*Batman Returns* Casts Jews as a Force for Evil."

A Jewish reader who initially assumed the article could be dismissed as the "product of a pair of intellectually overheated, pretentiously affected, and politically correct undergraduates straining to ferret out nonexistent sinister motives," became a convert after seeing the "vile motion picture."[2] He was puzzled why it hadn't been censored in the production process.

After positing this taken-for-granted censorship regime, he inconsistently concluded that *Batman Returns* "gives the lie to the shibboleth that Jews control the entertainment industry and use it to manipulate the American public."

Even paleoconservatives felt compelled to weigh in on behalf of the weak, ever-persecuted Jews.

Chronicles magazine's contribution to the dialogue was "Christmastime in Hollywood" (December 1992) by David R. Slavitt, a derivative review reproducing the opinions of the Columbia undergraduates nearly verbatim.

"These Columbia kids," Slavitt averred, "are not crazy. If anything, their report is cautious, modest, and generally understated." Although it was hard to believe "that an industry from which the Jews are not significantly excluded" (!) would "base a surefire summer hit on the old blood libel," nevertheless, *Batman Returns* is "an old-fashioned 1930s Jew-baiting movie."

Since there *were* no 1930s "Jew-baiting" movies in America or virtually anywhere else, he was undoubtedly referring to Germany.

"The trouble with the Penguin," Slavitt sermonized, "is that his bestiality runs riot and that he outwardly proclaims it: 'I am not a human being! I am an animal!' Which is the fundamental basis of all bigotry—that *they* are not like *us* and in fact are not even human." "The Penguin," he concluded, "is at least as Jewish as Roiphe and Cooper claim." In summation:

The message from *Batman Returns* is that all our

---

[2] http://www.nytimes.com/1992/07/20/opinion/l-anti-semitism-in-batman-returns-be-serious-gratuitous-bigotry-120792.html

ills arise from the work of some small but evil bunch of rich and powerful people who are different from us—not quite human, beasts, vermin—and are therefore after blood, wanting to kill our children and our God.

Note that this outlook is, without qualification, exactly the way Jews demonize whites!

The movie left Slavitt feeling "dismayed" and "numb." He hinted darkly that a pogrom (or worse) might be in the offing.

A not exactly earth-shattering observation by Slavitt was that the film had an Expressionist look. (This is true of virtually all of Burton's films.) Expressionism was common in the German cinema of the Weimar era. The implication seemed to be that this, too, was somehow anti-Semitic.

Although the production designer for *Batman Returns* was Bo Welch, he inherited his expressionist designs from *Batman* (1989). The set designer for that film was British-born Jew Anton Furst, who committed suicide before the second project went into production by leaping from an LA parking garage.

Designer Bo Welch did mention in an interview that he had blended "Fascist architecture with World's Fair architecture" for Gotham City, and studied Russian architecture and German Expressionism.

ANTI-SEMITIC ALLEGORY?

Were the Jews right? Was *Batman Returns* an anti-Semitic allegory? Or were these aspects of the film some sort of odd coincidence?

When I saw *Batman Returns* I was well-versed about the Jewish problem, but did not automatically think, "This film is anti–Semitic!"

That doesn't mean such themes weren't present, but

until they were pointed out by anti-white writers they did not register with a racially conscious person such as myself. And, unlike me, most Gentiles are unaware.

There is another film that works better as anti-Jewish allegory.

That is John Carpenter's low budget sci-fi flick *They Live* (1988). Carpenter, who is white, is a typical Hollywood denizen. His objective was to discredit Reaganism and free enterprise. The film also prominently features a hoary propaganda cliché, the white-Negro "buddy" team (*The Defiant Ones*, Mel Gibson's *Lethal Weapon* series).

I have never seen *They Live* attacked as anti-Semitic by Jews the way *Batman Returns* was. Rather, I first read that take on the movie in 1988 in the now-defunct Populist Party's magazine *The Populist Observer*, and have seen many pro-white writers make the same point since.

In *They Live* the (unintended) anti-Jewish theme sticks out like a sore thumb for conscious whites in a way that it does not in *Batman Returns*. But the depiction of the Penguin in *Batman Returns* unquestionably set off the Jews' own alarm bells.

The anti-Jewish elements in *Batman Returns* might have been as unconscious and unintentional as Carpenter's were.

Another approach is to ask who made the film. Whose sensibilities, conscious and unconscious, does it express?

The corporate parent was media colossus Time Warner, run by Jews Steven J. Ross (real name Steven J. Rechnitz) and Gerald M. Levin.

The co-head of subsidiary production company Warner Brothers was Jew Terry Semel, later CEO of Internet giant Yahoo!.

Of the movie's six producers (director Tim Burton was one), Peter Guber and Benjamin Melnicker were Jewish, while New Jersey-born Michael Uslan's ethnicity is unknown. Apparent Gentiles were Jon Peters, supposedly half-Italian and half-Amerindian, and Denise Di Novi, a presumptive Italian-American.

Daniel Waters wrote the screenplay. Unfortunately for anti-white conspiracy theorists, his screenplay was heavily rewritten prior to filming by Wesley Strick, who is Jewish. Strick has been credited with authorship of two-thirds of the final script, including the Old Testament allusions.

As an aside, the final script reveals one way Hollywood scriptwriters, directors, and actors employ buzzwords to quickly convey white racial images and stereotypes to one another during production. In one scene I saw references to nameless characters including "ALL-AMERICAN DAD," "ALL-AMERICAN MOM," "ALL-AMERICAN SON," and "ADORABLE LITTLE GIRL" with her "precious little purse."

TIM BURTON

A movie's director ordinarily exercises more control than anyone else over the final product in terms of story, look, theme, etc. Counter-Currents and TOO film analyst Edmund Connelly relies upon "auteur theory"—the theory that the director is the main "author" of a film—in his readings of Hollywood movies. He succinctly summarizes that theory here.[3]

Tim Burton exercised considerable control over the making of *Batman Returns*.

His previous *Batman* (1989), the first film in the series, was one of the biggest box office hits of all time, grossing over $411 million. It won critical acclaim and an Academy Award for Best Art Direction. The success of the movie helped establish Burton as a profitable director.

During production, Burton had repeatedly clashed with the film's producers, Jon Peters and Peter Guber. But after the success of *Batman*, Warner Brothers wanted him

---

[3] http://www.theoccidentalobserver.net/2012/05/how-they-lie-to-us-the-film-margin-call/

to direct the sequel. He finally agreed on the condition that he be granted total control. As a result, producers Jon Peters and Peter Guber were demoted to executive producers.

Tim Burton has always seemed hyper-Jewish to me. (By my definition, half- and quarter-Jews are also "Jewish."[4]) Indeed, I find it nearly impossible to believe that he isn't. He is so strange, so alien, that next to him Alfred Hitchcock looks like Ward Cleaver.

But if Burton is Jewish, he is *extremely* crypto-.

The media implicitly presents Burton to the public as white. Reporters state that he was born in 1958 in Burbank, California to Jean Burton (*née* Erickson), the owner of a cat-themed gift shop, and Bill Burton, a former minor league baseball player who subsequently worked for the Burbank Park and Recreation Department.

Yet Tim Burton's background remains obscure. As late as the 1990s a newswriter incorrectly identified him as a "British director," and years ago I read that he was adopted.

He does not look Aryan.

His sensibility—notably his weirdness, obsessions, and conspicuous neuroticism—does not seem Aryan, either.

Burton's "art," whether his commercial films or the paintings, drawings, photographs, etc., featured in a retrospective at New York's Museum of Modern Art, does not look Aryan. Proof of all of this is on display in a 7:00-minute YouTube interview with Burton posted by the Museum of Modern Art in 2009 that highlights examples of his artwork.[5]

In 2003, a Jewish website no longer in existence listed

---

[4] https://www.counter-currents.com/2011/12/jews-and-whiteness/

[5] http://www.youtube.com/watch?v=mANsedYvsBs

Burton as Jewish,[6] and of 515 voters at a contemporary Jewish site called *Guess Who's the Jew?*, 58% thought him Jewish and 42% non-Jewish.[7] The site does not *verify* that he is in fact Jewish, but rather tabulates the perceptions of visitors.

Burton's amazing career trajectory suggests favoritism. He became a leading director of big budget movies while still in his 20s.

His career received major boosts from Disney Studios, where he was employed as an animator (gauge his qualification for commercial Disney animation work in the YouTube clip), and Warner Brothers, which gave him his first significant break directing *Pee Wee's Big Adventure* (1985) starring Pee-Wee Herman (Paul Reubens, born Paul Reubenfeld).

Burton's current mistress is actress Helena Bonham Carter. Nearly half Jewish, Bonham Carter has a complicated family tree, the product of hybridization between members of the British aristocracy and Europe's Jewish aristocracy. Burton has two children by her.

Finally, despite the toxic charges of anti-Semitism, Burton's career did not miss a beat. He was not unceremoniously cashiered like Mel Gibson and Charlie Sheen. That's too bad, because a suffering world would have been spared much ugly cultural dreck if he had been.

Self-Image

That from a Jewish perspective there are coded "anti-Jewish" messages in *Batman Returns* is interesting.

More interesting, though, is the fact that the controversy over them has completely disappeared from public view.

As John Derbyshire observed in connection with Wil-

---

[6] http://jewishpeople.net/famousjewssz.html
[7] http://www.guesswhosthejew.com/Tim_Burton.html

liam Cash's much-reviled 1994 *Spectator* (UK) article, "The Kings of the Deal".[8] "'It's surprising what you can find on the internet,' we used to say when the thing was new. Nowadays I am more often surprised by what I can't find on the internet."[9]

This is certainly true of *Batman Returns*. The 1992 assaults on the movie are conspicuously absent from the World Wide Web, especially given how prevalent they were at the time. Googling David Slavitt's *Chronicles* article does not turn up a single reference.

Perhaps some subjects are routinely downplayed or concealed by slyly jiggering search results. I can think of a particular search formula I consistently used with great success for many years that no longer works. The ADL partners with Jewish mega-giants Google and Facebook to censor Internet content on ideological and racial grounds. Such control of information choke points confers tremendous power.

Today most people do not know that such accusations were ever made, although oblique hints linger. For example, Jewish movie critic Leonard Maltin's bestselling annual *Movie Guide* gives *Batman Returns* only two stars, calling it, without explanation, a "nasty, nihilistic, nightmare movie" with a "dark, mean-spirited screenplay"—an obvious allusion to the Jewish themes discussed here.

But those who self-righteously take umbrage over alleged anti-Semitism in *Batman Returns* deserve no sympathy. They should have their faces shoved into anti-Semitism every bit as vicious and unrelenting as the anti-white filth *they* propagate daily without remorse, and experience the resultant violence and hatred as well. Such

---

[8] http://www.johnderbyshire.com/Opinions/Culture/Extras/KingsOfTheDeal/page.html

[9] http://www.vdare.com/articles/john-derbyshire-on-the-ballistic-trajectory-of-political-correctness

vile people are in no position to preach.

That won't happen, of course, but it should.

Surely the most extraordinary aspect of the entire affair, however, is that Jewish elites gazed upon the physically, psychologically, and morally deformed Penguin and instantly saw themselves.

"That's *us*!" they cried. "They're depicting us!"

Counter-Currents/*North American New Right*,
June 22, 2012

INDEX

A
A Tale of Two Cities, 60
Affleck, Ben, 68, 142, 145
Alberich, 193
Alda, Alan, 123
Allen, Barry, 147
Alt Right, 6, 116, 151, 155, 160, 163
Amazons, 147
American History X, 26
Amis, Kingsley, 118f., 121
Amis, Martin, 123
anarchy, 22, 176
anti-psychiatric movement, 170
anti-Semitism, 53, 191–200
Apollo, 112, 154
Apollonian, 67, 182, 185, 187, 189
Aquaman, 147–48
architecture, 97, 181, 183, 195
Aristotle, 85–86
Arkham Asylum, 62, 153, 161, 162, 168, 169–73
Arkham Asylum: A Serious House on Serious Earth, 169–75
Armenian Genocide, 94n7
Assassins (Islamic cult), 70
assimilation, 131, 192
Atlanteans, 147
Aurora, Colorado, 27, 40
auteur theory, 197
authenticity, 17

Avenger, heroic (archetype), 109, 167–68
Avengers, the (Marvel characters), 84
Avengers, The (Marvel movie), 40, 50, 55

B
Babylon, 67
Bacon, Francis, 187
Bacon-Smith, Camille, 190
Bakunin, 172
Bale, Christian, 11, 27, 123
Bane, 3, 5–6, 8, 9, 27, 31, 34–37, 42–49, 52–63, 68, 69, 70, 101, 112–14, 124n8, 125, 152
Basinger, Kim, 188
Bat Signal, 44, 49, 76
Bat Suit, 123, 125
Batcave, 44, 102, 188
Batcave (London nightclub), 184
Batgirl, 123
Batman (Tim Burton film), 181–90, 191, 195, 197
Batman (TV series), 185
"Batman and the Jewish Question," 191
Batman Begins, 2, 4, 11–14, 15, 18, 26, 27, 28, 31, 46, 70, 74, 98, 105–106, 108, 113
Batman Mythos, 3, 67, 79
Batman Returns, 191–201

Batman: The Dark Knight Returns (animated movie), 161–64
Batman Trilogy; see Dark Knight Trilogy
Batman v Superman: Dawn of Justice, 109, 141–45, 146, 163
Batmobile, 13, 44, 167
Battlestar Galactica, 126–27
Bauhaus (musical group), 183
Beati Paoli, 84
behaviorism, 170
Being, 23–24, 32–33
being, interpretation of, 23–24
Benn, Gottfried, 173
Bickle, Travis, 26
"Big Blue Boy Scout," 8, 131
Big Hollywood, 52–53, 60, 62–63, 65
Bill the Butcher, 26
Black Lives Matter, 154
Blackgate Prison, 60
Black-mask, 170
Blake, Robin John, 1–2, 6–7, 27, 38, 43–44, 49, 64, 102, 161, 162
Blofeld, Ernst Stavro, 121
Bloom, Allan, 77n1
bodybuilding, 122–25
Bogart, Humphrey, 173
Bolsheviks, 84, 127
Bond, James, 55, 118f.
Bonham-Carter, Helena, 199
Boreanaz, David, 11
bourgeois society, 183, 187–89

Bowden, Jonathan, 189
Bowie, David, 124
Brave and the Bold, The, 165–68
Breitbart, Andrew, 52
Broadmoor, 169
Bronx, The, 120
Buffalo Bill (fictional serial killer), 123
Burton, Tim, 181–201

C

Caddyshack, 50
Caesar, Julius, 73, 74, 95–103
Caesarism, 101, 103
Caine, Michael, 11, 27, 57, 97
Caligula (play), 172
Caligula (Roman emperor), 172
camaraderie, 171
Cameron, James, 91
Camus, Albert, 172
cannibalism, 36, 170
Caped Crusader, 3, 65, 106, 160, 179, 185n5
capitalism, 2, 53, 55, 60, 121, 189
Carpenter, John, 196
Cash, William, 199
Casino Royale, 120
Catwoman, 6, 27, 34, 37, 42, 63, 191
Cavill, Henry, 136, 145
Céline, Louis-Ferdinand, 173
chaos, 4, 13, 22–25, 55, 58, 81, 104, 112, 149, 152, 154, 158, 163

Index

Charlemagne Division (SS), 175
Chicago, 67
China, 11, 12, 28, 103, 108
chivalry, 110–11
Christianity, 135–36, 139
Christmas, 193–94
"Christmastime in Hollywood," 194
Christopher Nolan Trilogy; see Dark Knight Trilogy
Chronicles, 194, 200
CIA, 46
Class: A Guide Through the American Status System, 120
classicism, 181, 187
Clay Face, 170, 175
Clean Slate, 34, 37
Cleaver, Ward, 198
Clooney, George, 11, 123
Cohen, Leonard, 149
Cold War, The, 117, 150–51
Comics Code Authority, 151, 167–69
Conan the Barbarian, 156
Concerned Professors, 171
Connelly, Edmund, 197
Conservative Revolutionaries, 7, 8, 171
conservatives, 7, 52, 58, 60, 64, 65; see also paleoconservatives
conservativism, 51, 61, 65, 151, 155
conspiracy theories, 91, 197
Constantinople, 28, 46
consuls, 87
contingency, 23–26
Cooper, Daniel, 191

Corto Maltese, 162, 163
cosmic order, 2, 8, 28
Costner, Kevin, 126
Cotillard, Marion, 27
Craig, Daniel, 121
Crane, Dr. Jonathan, 7, 43, 47, 62, 69, 98
Crisis of the Modern World, The, 116
Croc (villain), 170, 175
Crowe, Russell, 132
Cruz, Ted, 150
crypsis, 83, 127, 198
Cure, The, 183
Cyborg (character), 147–48

D

Dagget, John, 56–59
Damned, the, 183
Dark Age, 12, 14, 28; see also Kali Yuga
Dark Ages, 181, 189
Dark Enlightenment, 189
Dark Knight Returns, The (graphic novel), 9, 141, 150–61
Dark Knight Rises, The, 2, 8, 27–38, 39–50, 51, 53, 66, 70, 84, 95, 101–102, 105, 113, 116, 124n8, 152
Dark Knight Trilogy, 2–5, 7–8, 27–28, 39–40, 45, 49–51, 64, 67, 95, 98, 101–105, 108, 115, 126, 145
Dark Knight, The, 3, 4, 11, 15–26, 27–28, 30, 33–36, 41, 61, 70–76, 88, 95, 98–99, 102, 105, 108, 110, 142, 154, 165
Das Rheingold, 193

Dasein, 188
Dawes, Rachel, 4, 5, 19, 21–22, 31, 38, 41–42, 45, 71–74, 76, 100, 109
DC Comics, Inc., 165, 169
death (and authenticity), 17–25
decadence, 12–13, 35, 96, 113–14
Decline of the West, The, 103n2
deep state, 83–94
Defiant Ones, The, 196
Degas, Edgar, 187
del Toro, Guillermo, 14
democracy, 64, 72–73, 75, 79, 81, 88, 91, 100, 108, 112–13, 121, 157–58
Democrat Party, 52–53
Dent, Harvey, 3–5, 17, 19–23, 30–31, 37–43, 60, 62, 73–75, 88, 100, 109, 111–13, 154, 162, 189
Dent Act, 31, 40, 43, 62
Derbyshire, John, 199–200
despair, 60, 113
Detective Comics, 178
DeVito, Danny, 191
Di Novi, Denise, 197
Dickens, Charles, 60
dictator (Roman office), 88
Dionysian, 182, 187
Dionysus, 154
Disney Studios, 199
diversity, 129
DNA, 24, 33, 139; see also genetic code
Doctor Destiny, 170, 175
Donner, Richard, 126, 186
Donovan, Jack, 160
Doom, Thulsa, 156
Doonesbury, 177
Douthat, Ross, 54–55
Downey, Robert, 124
Dracula (character), 192
Dracula (Stoker novel), 189
Draper, Don, 119n4, 124
Drax, Hugo, 118
Drieu La Rochelle, 173
dualism, 165, 169, 175
Ducard, Henri, 12–13, 28, 68–70, 74; see also Ra's al Ghul

E
Earle, William, 69
Eckhart, Aaron, 21
effeminacy, 163, 173
egalitarianism, 6, 8, 15, 26, 32, 36, 37, 47, 51, 55, 63, 110, 129, 132, 140; see also equality
eidos, 68
Eisenberg, Jesse, 142, 145
Elders of Zion, 83
Elfman, Danny, 187, 193
elites, 106, 110, 159, 177, 201
Ellison, Harlan, 178
enlightenment, 62, 181
equality, 6, 13, 41, 51, 53, 59, 108, 110, 129, 155, 177; see also egalitarianism
equity (*epieikeia*), 86n4
Erdogan, Recip, 91
Ereignis, 24–25
ethnic networking, 116
eugenics, 80, 128–29
Eurocentrism, 182
Europe, 154, 158, 181, 187
European New Right, 65

Index 207

evil, 5, 8, 32–33, 40, 48, 51–53, 56, 61, 109, 111, 135, 141, 176–80, 183, 191–93, 195
Evola, Julius, 14
exception, state of, 84–90
existentialism, 17, 172
Exodus (Biblical book), 191, 192

F
Facebook, 12, 200
Falcone, Carmine, 2, 68, 95, 98, 106
Family Guy, 122
fascism, 38, 48, 51–53, 64, 68, 107–108, 115, 153, 156, 160, 165, 168, 172–73, 175, 195
fate, 62, 101, 139, 175
fatherhood, 171
Faustianism, 126
Fellowship of the Ring, The, 147
Film Noir, 183, 186
Finch, Senator June, 142
Finger, Bill, 184
Flash, The, 147–48
Florence, 49, 64, 102, 120n5
football game, 34, 43, 47, 59, 124n8
Founders (American), 90
Fox, Lucius, 74, 108
Fox News, 63
Franklin, Benjamin, 182
Fredersen, Freder, 187
freedom, 7, 16–25, 34, 43, 48, 60, 90
Freeman, Morgan, 11, 14, 27
Freeze, Mr., 124

French Revolution, the, 139
Freudianism, 170
From Krakow to Krypton: Jews & Comic Books, 83n1
Furst, Anton, 195
Fussell, Paul, 120, 124
Fussell, S. W., 124n7

G
Gable, Don, 177–78
Gadot, Gal, 143, 145
Gainsborough, Thomas, 187
Gambol, 17, 18
Gangs of New York, 26
Gebirgsjäger, 2
genetic code, 128; see also DNA
genocide, 127, 130
German Expressionism, 183, 186, 192, 195
Germanization of Early Medieval Christianity, The, 134
Gestell, 23–26
Gibson, Mel, 196, 199
Giorgio Vasari, 181n1
globalism, 1, 84, 107, 159
Golden Age, 12, 14, 28
Goldman Sachs, 52
golem, 117
good and evil, 32–33, 40, 176, 183
Gordon, Commissioner James (Jim), 3–5, 24, 31, 33, 38, 41–44, 49, 72–76, 80, 84, 89, 98, 161, 166, 168, 174–75
Gordon-Leavitt, Joseph, 27

Gotham (village in Nottinghamshire, England), 184
Gotham City, 3, 12–15, 43, 61, 63, 66, 73, 152, 184, 191, 193, 195
Gotham Police, 2, 62, 98
Gotham Police, 2, 61, 98
gothic rock, 183
Gothic (style), 181–89
Goyer, David, 14, 52, 126
goyim, 83, 116, 127, 132, 148
graphic novels, 9, 116, 149, 167
Graves, Robert, 172
Greenstreet, Sydney, 173
Grissom, Carl, 186
Guber, Peter, 198
guardians, 78–79
Guénon, René, 14, 116, 117, 121, 122
Guess Who's the Jew?, 198
Gyges, 77

H
Hardy, Tom, 27
Hathaway, Ann, 27, 42
Hauer, Rutger, 11
Heidegger, Martin, 23–24, 26, 140
Hellboy, 14, 83n2, 127
Hellboy II: The Golden Army, 14, 83n2, 127
Helms, Alan, 122
Hermes, 80–82; see also the trickster
hero's journey, 151
hierarchy, 55, 86, 129, 135
Hill, Benny, 178
history, 12, 14, 26, 28, 47, 52, 103–104, 150, 154, 158
Hitchcock, Alfred, 198
Hitler, Adolf, 52, 87–88, 157, 159, 173
Hollywood Kryptonite: The Bulldog, the Lady, and the Death of Superman, 117n2
Hollywood, 14, 25–26, 30, 39, 41, 116, 146, 148, 149, 167, 183, 189, 190, 194, 197
Holy Terror, 152
homoeroticism, 123
Hood, Gregory, 144
human rights, 13, 26
humanism, 29–30, 32–33, 37, 84, 127, 129, 164
Hunter, Holly, 142

I
immigration, 127, 152
Inception, 126
Indians (Pacific Northwest), 21
Indochina, 119n4
industrial (music genre), 183
initiation, 18, 29, 31–33, 37, 49
innocence, 56, 59
Iron Man, 117, 119, 124
Irredeemable, 131, 139
Irving, Washington, 184
Islam, 68, 154
Islamists, 69, 91
Israel, 164
Italy, 34

J
Jackson, Peter, 143

Index

James Bond Dossier, The, 118f.
Jews, 83, 92–93, 127–30, 131–37, 145, 148, 156, 158, 162–64, 191, 193–98; see also Organized Jewry
jihadists, 106
Joker, the, 3–5, 7, 11, 15–26, 30, 33–36, 41, 56, 75, 81, 98–101, 108–15, 142, 153–55, 162–74, 184–89
Jor-El, 128, 132–34, 137–39
Jung, C. G., 97–101, 182, 188
Jünger, Ernst, 173
justice, 2–4, 8–9, 29–30, 40, 56–58, 61, 67–68, 77, 82, 84–89, 104, 108–114, 131, 149, 157
Justice League (characters), 67, 83, 147–48
Justice League (film), 146–49

K
Kane, Bob, 184, 185n5
Kansas, 67, 138, 144
Kant, Immanuel, 182
Kashner, Sam, 117n2
Keaton, Michael, 11, 123, 188, 191
Kelley, Carrie, 162
Kennedy, John, 119n4
Kent, Clark, 67, 134, 136, 142, 144, 157
Kent, Jonathan, 134
Kent, Martha, 143
Kersey, Paul (blogger), 124n8
Keystone Cops, 178
Killing Joke, The, 99, 176

Kilmer, Val, 11, 123
"Kings of the Deal, The," 199f.
Knight (archetype), 40, 76, 106–107, 111–13
Kristol, Bill, 53
Krypton, 128–29, 138, 143
Kryptonite, 142–45, 163
Ku Klux Klan, 84
Kürten, Peter, 171
Kyle, Selina, 6, 8, 34, 42–45, 47–48, 49, 53, 63–64, 102

L
LA (Los Angeles), 107, 195
Lane, Lois, 137, 142–43
Lang, Fritz, 171, 186
Lau, Mr., 20, 68, 108
Lauren, Ralph, 120
Lawrence, D. H., 173
Lawrence, T. E., 173
League of Shadows, 2, 4–5, 7, 12–13, 15, 18, 26–32, 38, 42, 44, 46, 48, 50, 56–63, 68, 70, 94–98, 101, 105, 109–13, 121, 124; see also the order
Lebensraum, 129
Lecter, Dr. Hannibal, 120n5
Ledger, Heath, 4, 11, 15, 25
Left, the, 38, 51, 60, 65, 106–107, 159, 177, 180, 182, 187
Leftism, 8, 38
Leonardo Da Vinci, 185
lesbians, 162, 173
Lethal Weapon series, 196
Levin, Gerald M., 196
Lewis, Wyndham, 173

liberalism, 48, 88, 89, 91, 105–108
lies, 37–38, 41, 43, 64, 80
Limbaugh, Rush, 53
Linkola, Pentti, 13
Lion Sheik, the, 154
Lipshitz, Ralph, 120
Lives of the Artists, The, 181n1
Locke, John, 182
Lohengrin, 193
Loki, 55, 135
London, 96, 124, 148, 184
Lower East Side (New York City), 132
Luthor, Lex, 142–146, 148, 176
Lynch, Trevor, 4, 83n2, 127n1, 146n1, 165

M
"M" (Bond character), 121
M (Fritz Lang film), 171
Mad Hatter, 170
Mad Men, 119n4, 124
Madonna, 122
mafia, the, 3, 68, 176; see also the mob, organized crime
Maltese Falcon, The (film), 173
Maltin, Leonard, 200
Man of Steel, 156, 159; see also Superman
Man of Steel, 83n2, 126–40, 141–42, 144, 146
Manicheanism, 167, 169
Maria (character), 187
Maroni, Sal "Boss," 68
martial arts, 39, 106

masked vigilantes, 49, 73, 84f., 152
Maxie Zeus, 170
McKean, Dave, 169, 174
Mefistofele (opera), 95
Melnicker, Benjamin, 196
messianic figure, 100–102, 134
metahumans, 144
Methodism, 134
Metropolis, 186–87
militarism, 135
Miller, Frank, 9, 141, 150–60, 161, 164, 185, 185n6
Mishima, Yukio, 173
Mitchum, Robert, 122
mob (criminal) vs. mob (masses), 70–71
mob, the, 2, 7, 16, 20, 22, 71–76, 79, 106, 108; see also mafia, organized crime
modernity, 23, 39, 41, 51, 66, 187
money (contempt for), 15–21, 34–35, 46, 56, 58–59, 70–71, 98, 101, 177
Money (novel), 123
monsters, 5, 16, 25–26, 30, 35, 177
morality, 4, 13, 16, 18, 20, 21, 23, 26, 29, 30, 35, 36, 84, 108, 110, 111, 127, 129, 131, 134, 139, 188, 192
Morpheus, 126
Morris, Dick, 53
Morrison, Grant, 169, 173, 174
Moses, 128, 191, 192
mother boxes, 147

multiculturalism, 127, 159
Murnau, F. W., 192
Murphy, Cillian, 11, 27
Muscle: Confessions of an Unlikely Bodybuilder, 124n7
Museum of Modern Art (NYC), 198
Mutants, the, 156, 161, 162
Mysteries of Udolpho, The, 189
Mystery Science Theater 3000, 122
myth of metals, 80
mythos, 1; see also Batman mythos

N
Napier, Jack, 186; see also the Joker
National Anthem, 47, 59
National Film Theatre (UK), 173
National Periodical Publications, 165
NATO, 119
Nazis (National Socialists), 52, 53, 84, 127, 129, 131, 132, 141
Neeson, Liam, 11–13, 28
neocons, 84, 156, 164
Neo-Realism, Italian, 173
New Left, 182
New Wave (music genre), 183
New York, 26, 67, 81, 96, 107, 122, 163, 184
New York Law School, 191
New York Times, 54, 191
Nicholson, Jack, 120

Nicomachean Ethics, 86n4
Nibelungen, 193
Nietzsche, Friedrich, 13, 15, 26, 32, 39, 52, 109, 111, 126, 133, 141, 156, 158, 172, 174, 182
"Night of Thanks, but no Thanks!, The" 178f.
nihilism and nihilists, 38, 54, 55–56, 58, 60, 65, 166, 189, 200
Niven, David, 120
noble lie, 5, 64, 76, 79–81
Nolan, Christopher, 1–9, 11, 14, 15, 27, 38, 39, 40, 47, 51–54, 59–60, 65–66, 68–71, 74, 76, 79, 82, 84, 88, 95, 101, 105, 108–109, 111, 115, 126, 145, 146, 154, 185
Nolan, Jonathan, 52
Nolte, John, 52–55, 57
Northern England, 183
Northwestern Europe, 181
Nosferatu, 192

O
O'Hehir, Andrew, 51
O'Meara, James J., 30
Obama, Barack, 53–55, 106, 120
Obama, Michelle, 120
Occidental Observer, The, 197
Occupy Wall Street, 47, 48, 54, 70, 152
Odin, 135, 175
Office of Special Plans, 83
Official Preppy Handbook, The, 120

Oldman, Gary, 11, 27
order, the, 42, 46, 48, 57–59, 67; see also League of Shadows
organized crime, 3, 5, 30, 40, 67–73, 95; see also the mob, the mafia
organized Jewry, 92–93; see also Jews

P

pagans, 67, 136, 175
paleoconservatives, 194; see also conservatives
parademons, 147
Paris Commune, 43
Parker, Peter, 119
paternalism, 171, 189
Pavel, Dr. Leonid, 62
Pearl Harbor, 164
Pee Wee's Big Adventure, 199
Pee-Wee Herman, 199
Penguin, the, 176, 191–94, 201
Pennyworth, Alfred, 2, 5–7, 25, 31, 38, 42–45, 57, 63, 70–71, 74, 76, 81, 97–98, 102, 163, 180
Peters, Jon, 197, 198
Pfeiffer, Michelle, 191
Philosopher King, 78
Plato, 5, 76–82, 86n1, 133
Plutonian, the, 139
Political Theology: Four Chapters on the Concept of Sovereignty, 85n3
Populist Observer, The, 196
pornography, 127

post-Enlightenment, 182, 183, 187
potlatch, 21
Pound, Ezra, 173
pre-Enlightenment, 189
Prince (pop star), 187
Prince, Diana, 67
Princeton, 12
Professor Milo, 170, 175
progress, 12, 14–15, 26, 38, 113, 177
Project for a New American Century, 83
psychoanalysis, 127
psychopathy, 170–71
Punisher, the, 131

Q

"Q" (Bond character), 120

R

Ra's al Ghul, 1–6, 12–13, 18, 20, 26, 28, 29, 42, 44, 46, 49, 57, 58, 60, 62, 69, 75, 95, 96, 98, 101–103, 108–12, 114; see also Ducard, Henri
Radcliffe, Ann, 189
Radical Traditionalism, 39, 50; see also Traditionalism
Raffles (character), 121
rape, 154, 170, 171, 177
Reagan, Ronald, 65, 162–63
Reaganism, 196
Rechnitz, Stephen J., 196
Red Son, 131
Reeve, Christopher, 117
Reeves, George, 117, 122
Reichstag, 87

Rembrandt, 187
Renaissance, 181
Renoir, Auguste, 187
Republic, The, 76–79, 86n4, 133
Republicans, 40, 53, 55
Resurrection, 144
Reubenfeld, Paul, 199
Reubens, Paul, 199
Riddler, 20
Robin, 1, 6–7, 27, 38, 44, 49, 64, 84, 102, 123, 161–62
Robin Hood, 84
Roiphe, Anne, 191
Roiphe, Rebecca, 191, 195
Roman Empire, 181
Rome, 28, 46, 67, 96, 103, 158
Romney, Mitt, 47, 53
Roosevelt, Franklin Delano, 164
Rorschach tests, 170
Ross, Stephen J., 196
Rotwang, 187
Russell, James, 135

S
sacrifice, 7–8, 19, 30, 45, 49, 52, 62–65, 87, 89, 93, 102–103, 134–35, 137–38, 144
Sallis, Ted, 83n1
salvation, 139, 144
Sapper (pen name of H. C. McNeile), 121
SAS (Special Air Services), 2, 120
Satya Yuga, 28; see also Golden Age
Savitri Devi, 14

Scarecrow, the, 3, 7, 43, 62, 69, 98, 170, 175
schemers, 22, 26, 41
schizophrenia, 170
Schmitt, Carl, 84–93, 164
Schumacher, Joel, 123
"Schwan der Scheldt," 193
Schwarzenegger, Arnold, 91, 122, 124
Scott, George C., 158
Second World War, 156, 173
secret societies, 91
Semel, Terry, 196
Serrano, Miguel, 14
Sex and Character, 174
shadow (Jungian), 98, 100, 155, 182, 188
Shadow, The (pulp magazine and radio show), 167
Shapiro, Ben, 52–55, 57
Shatner, William, 27, 117
Sheen, Charlie, 199
Shreck, Max (character), 191–93
Shreck, Max (German actor), 192
Shuster, Joe, 128, 156
Siegel, Jerry, 128, 156
Silence of the Lambs, 120n5, 123
Singapore, 139
Sisters of Mercy, the (musical group), 183
Slade (character), 166–68
Slavitt, David R., 194–95, 200
Smails, Judge Elihu, 50
SMERSH, 121

Snyder, Autumn, 146
Snyder, Zack, 15, 109, 126–27, 132, 135–49, 163
Social Darwinism, 129
social workers, 171
socialists (egalitarian), 48, 58, 60
soldiers, 22, 92, 141, 164
Sons of Batman (vigilantes), 156, 158, 162–63
Southern Europe, 181
Southern Poverty Law Center, 54
sovereignty, 83–94
Spartans, 87
Spectator (UK), 199
Spengler, Oswald, 96, 97, 101, 103, 104
Spider Man, 117
Star Wars, 55
Stark, Tony, 119, 124
Starling, Clarice (FBI agent), 120n5, 123
Steampunk, 183, 186
Steppenwolf (character), 147
Stirner, Max, 166, 172
stock exchange, 34, 46–47, 53, 58
Stoker, Bram, 189
Stone, Victor, 147
Strauss, Leo, 64
Strick, Wesley, 191, 197
Sucker Punch, 127, 145–46
super sanity, 172
superheroes, 1, 7, 9, 49, 64, 83–94, 105, 114, 115, 127–29, 143, 145, 150, 186
Superman (1978), 186
Superman (archetype), 13, 16, 33, 39, 132, 158, 160, 165, 174; see also *Übermensch*
Superman (character), 8, 13, 40, 117–18, 122, 126–49, 150, 153, 156–60, 162–63, 165, 176, 186
supervillains, 84, 127–28, 148
syndicate, 3, 71, 98; see also the mob; the mafia; organized crime
system, the, 4, 5, 8, 19, 24–26, 64, 91–93, 105, 110, 112

T
Talia (a.k.a. Tate, Miranda), 6, 27, 44–48, 56
tarot, 175
Tate, Miranda (a.k.a. Talia), 27, 41, 43, 44, 58
Taxi Driver, 26
They Live, 196
Thrasymachus, 77
Thunderball, 119
Thus Spoke Zarathustra, 156
Time Warner, 196
titans, 175
Todd, Jason, 161, 164
torture, 6, 61, 77, 171
Tourette's syndrome, 171–72
Traditionalism, 4, 7–8, 14, 26, 28, 32, 39–40, 48, 50, 57–60, 63, 65–66, 110, 114, 121, 135, 148, 183; see also Radical Traditionalism

transcendence, 1, 78, 103, 126, 175
transvaluation of values, 16, 18f.
transvestism, 173
trauma, 11–12, 29–32
trickster, 80–82, 98–101; see also Hermes
Trickster Makes This World (Hyde), 81n5
Trudeau, Gary, 177
True Lies, 91
True Prep: It's a Whole New Old World, 120
Trump, Donald J., 150
Truth, Justice, and the American Way, 67, 131, 157
Turkey, 91
Tweedle-Dum and Tweedle-Dee, 170
Twilight, 143
Twin Towers (Gotham City), 153
Two-Face, 5, 22–23, 30, 40, 75, 109, 112, 153, 155, 162, 170, 175, 189

U
Übermensch, 13, 15, 30, 68, 156; see also Superman (archetype)
Unabomber, 16
Uncle Sam, 156
Uslan, Michael, 196

V
Vale, Vicki, 187–88
Vedanta, 32–33
Vendicatori, 84
Victorianism, 183

Vinyard, Derek, 26
virtue-signaling, 157
virtus, 106

W
Wagner, Richard, 52, 193
Walken, Christopher, 191
War of 1812, 158
Warner Brothers, 146, 197, 199
warrior ethos, 110–11
Washington, D.C., 67
Watanabe, Ken, 11, 12
Watchmen, 15, 105, 126–27, 132, 144, 146, 149
Waters, Daniel, 197
Wayne, Bruce, 1–13, 18, 28–31, 34, 37–45, 47, 49, 53, 57–65, 67–74, 78, 81, 88, 95–100, 104, 106, 109–12, 120–21, 142–43, 147, 152, 154, 155, 159–64, 172, 178, 180, 185, 187–88
Wayne, Thomas, 2, 7, 69
Wayne Enterprises, 2, 31, 41, 43, 46, 58, 69
Wayne Manor, 7, 31, 47, 49, 72, 97, 163, 188
Wayne Tower, 97
wealth, 8, 20–21, 78, 92–93, 97, 102, 106
Weimar Constitution, 87
Weimar Republic, 171, 195
Weininger, Otto, 174
weird (wyrd), 175
Welch, Bo, 195
Welles, Orson, 167
West, Adam, 11, 117, 123
Whedon, Joss, 146–47
White Christ, the, 131–40

White Nationalists, 38, 39, 92–94, 105
will, 111–14
Will to Power, 18, 114
Williams, Billy Dee, 189
Wolper, Dr. Bartholomew, 153–54, 162–63
Wonder Woman, 143–48

X
X-Men, 83
xenophobia, 127–29

Y
Yahoo!, 196
Yarbrough, Tyrone, 190
Yglesias, Matt, 51
Yindel, Ellen, 162, 164

Z
Zeitgeist, 24
Zimmer, Hans, 27, 129, 141
zionism, 127, 135
Zod, General, 128–29, 132–35, 137, 139

About the Authors

Jonathan Bowden (1962–2012) was the author of *Pulp Fascism: Right-Wing Themes in Comics, Graphic Novels, & Popular Literature* (Counter-Currents, 2013), *Western Civilization Bites Back* (Counter-Currents, 2014), *Extremists: Studies in Metapolitics* (Counter-Currents, 2017), and many other books.

Luke Gordon writes for Counter-Currents/*North American New Right*.

Andrew Hamilton is the author of many essays and reviews, principally for Counter-Currents/*North American New Right*.

Gregory Hood is the author of *Waking Up from the American Dream* (Counter-Currents, 2015) and many essays and reviews. He is a staff writer for *American Renaissance* (amren.com).

Greg Johnson, Ph.D. is the Editor-in-Chief of Counter-Currents Publishing and the author of *Confessions of a Reluctant Hater* (Counter-Currents, 2010; second, expanded ed., 2016), *New Right vs. Old Right* (Counter-Currents, 2013), *Truth, Justice, & a Nice White Country* (Counter-Currents, 2015), *In Defense of Prejudice* (Counter-Currents, 2017), and *You Asked for It: Selected Interviews*, vol. 1 (Counter-Currents, 2017).

Jason Reza Jorjani, Ph.D. is the author of *Prometheus & Atlas* (2016), *World State of Emergency* (2017), *Lovers of Sophia* (2017), and *Novel Folklore* (2018). His website is https://jasonrezajorjani.com/.

Trevor Lynch is a pen name of Greg Johnson and the author of *Trevor Lynch's White Nationalist Guide to the Movies* (Counter-Currents, 2012) and *Son of Trevor Lynch's White Nationalist Guide to the Movies* (Counter-Currents, 2015).

James J. O'Meara is the author of *The Homo & the Negro* (Counter-Currents, 2012; second, embiggened ed., 2017), *The Eldritch Evola ... & Others* (Counter-Currents, 2014), *End of an Era:* Mad Men *& the Ordeal of Civility* (Counter-Currents, 2015), and *Green Nazis in Space: New Essays on Literature, Art, & Culture* (Counter-Currents, 2015), as well as many other essays and reviews.

Christopher Pankhurst is the author of *Numinous Machines* (Counter-Currents, 2017).

Spencer J. Quinn is the author of *White Like You* (Counter-Currents, 2017) and *Reframing White Nationalism* (Counter-Currents, 2018).

Zachary O. Ray writes for Counter-Currents/*North American New Right*. His blog is *Plugging Out*, http://plugging-out.blogspot.com/2016/09/the-alt-knight-retrospect-of-frank.html

Will Windsor writes for Counter-Currents/*North American New Right*.

David Yorkshire is the editor of *Mjolnir Magazine*, https://mjolnirmagazine.blogspot.com, and the author of many essays and reviews.

www.ingramcontent.com/pod-product-compliance
Lightning Source LLC
Chambersburg PA
CBHW030342131224
18858CB00004B/133